T0159010

Our

MOTHER

Who Art in

HEAVEN

Raphael Obotama

authorHOUSE®

AuthorHouse™
1663 Liberty Drive
Bloomington, IN 47403
www.authorhouse.com
Phone: 1 (800) 839-8640

New American Standard Bible (NASB)
Copyright © 1960, 1962, 1963, 1968, 1971, 1972, 1973,
1975, 1977, 1995 by The Lockman Foundation

Published by AuthorHouse   09/14/2017

ISBN: 978-1-5462-0757-3 (sc)
ISBN: 978-1-5462-0758-0 (e)

Library of Congress Control Number: 2017913909

Print information available on the last page.

Any people depicted in stock imagery provided by Thinkstock are models,
and such images are being used for illustrative purposes only.
Certain stock imagery © Thinkstock.

This book is printed on acid-free paper.

DIOCESE OF BISMARCK

PO Box 1575
Bismarck, ND 58502-1575
Phone: 701-223-1347
Fax: 701-223-3693
www.bismarckdiocese.com

OFFICE OF THE BISHOP

DECREE

In accord with the norm of Ecclesiastical Law and the prescriptions of Canon 824§2, and Canon 827 of the Code of Canon Law, by these presents the undersigned Diocesan Bishop herewith grants the

Nihil Obstat and *Imprimatur*

for the book titled *Our Mother Who Art in Heaven* published by Author House, Bloomington, Indiana.

It is understood that the *Nihil Obstat* and *Imprimatur* are official declarations that a book or pamphlet is free of doctrinal or moral error. No implication is contained therein that those who have granted them agree with the content or statements expressed.

The Most Reverend David D. Kagan, D.D., P.A., J.C.L.
Bishop of Bismarck

Given at the Chancery this
29th day of June A.D. 2017

Mr. Dale Eberle
Chancellor

CONTENTS

ACKNOWLEDGMENT

I have to give glory to God first whose Holy Spirit inspires us, His Grace is truly sufficient for me. Our Lord Jesus Christ who promised to be with us always is still at work, may His name be praised. I thank the Blessed Virgin Mary my very special Mother who has proven herself a mother to me in every circumstance.

This book is a result of many hands coming together at one point or another and I have to acknowledge those who have in one way or the other helped me through the research, writing and publishing of this book.

On the human level my appreciation goes to Bishop David Kagan the bishop of Bismarck Catholic diocese in North Dakota who not only read the manuscript but also wrote the foreword for the book and also granted imprimatur and nihil obstat. I am also grateful to Bishop Camillus Umoh the bishop of Ikot Ekpene my home diocese for his fatherly encouragement all through these years. My appreciation also goes to Mary Januzs, Dr. Oscar Udoh, Dr. Mrs. Bridget Udoh, and Sr. Imelda Effiong HHCJ, who read through the manuscript and took time to offer very useful suggestions and encouraging feedback. Finally I remain grateful to my parents who made it a family tradition to say the rosary every day, a tradition that has helped me to be closer to the Blessed Virgin Mary.

FOREWORD

Our Mother Who Art In Heaven is offered to us as not only a pious reflection by Father Raphael Obotama, a devoted son of the Mother of God, but also as a good and useful synthesis of Roman Catholic doctrine and practice with regard to the Mother of the Divine Savior.

Father reliance on the abundant and rich references to Mary throughout the Sacred Scriptures and his consistent references to what our Roman Catholic Tradition continues to say and do with such loving reverence for her speaks volumes about Her place of primacy in the Communion of Saints and in the lived experience of Her children down through the ages and even to our own day.

In every chapter of this wonderful work, Father Obotama leads us through his own reflections to what the Catholic Church believes of Our Blessed Lady and what it practices spiritually and liturgically. Each chapter and each page of each chapter presents to us the lived faith of the Church from Apostolic times to the present and truly, until the end of time. It is Mary, the Mother of God, who not only shows us Jesus but leads us unconditionally in following Him if we so choose to do this. Pope Benedict XVI said in his sermon for the Solemnity of the Assumption in 2006: "And it is precisely by looking at Mary's face that we can see more clearly than in any other way the beauty, goodness and mercy of God. In her face we can truly perceive the divine light."

I found and I hope you find as well that Chapter 14 gives to this entire reflection that cohesiveness which is one of the hallmarks of Catholic Marian doctrine. The title itself gives us that same clarity, "Mary the Teacher and Evangelizer". From her fiat at the moment of the Annunciation which produced the Incarnation of God as man, to her final recorded words in the Gospels, "do whatever He tells you", to her prayerful and dynamic presence with the Twelve on that first Pentecost, Mary is herself the living school of Jesus Christ.

Again, Pope Benedict XVI has called her the star of evangelization. He said of her: "The Virgin Mary, who did not communicate to the world an idea but Jesus, the Incarnate Word, is an unparalleled model of evangelization" (Angelus, 12-23-2006). The following year Pope Benedict XVI said in his message for World Mission Sunday: "May she especially make us all aware of being missionaries, that is, those who have been sent out by the Lord to be his witnesses at every moment of our life" (5-27-2007).

May we all strive faithfully and daily to be the sons and daughters of Mary, Mother of God, Mother of the

Church, and Mother of us all by allowing Her to teach us of Jesus and by allowing Her to lead us in following Jesus. Like Her may we bring others with us through Her to Him.

The Most Reverend David D. Kagan
Bishop of Bismarck

Solemnity of Ss. Peter & Paul
29June 2017

INTRODUCTION

She was just a teenager, a virgin from Nazareth, when the God of her ancestors, the God of Israel, sent an emissary to her. The emissary, an angel, came to her, and without even introducing himself, gave the teenager an unusual greeting; "Hail, favored one, the Lord is with you."

She was shocked and confused; the heavenly visitor revealed that she was the most highly favored of all human beings. He announced that she'd been given the most onerous mission ever given to any human being: "You shall conceive in your womb and bear a son, who shall be called the Son of God." The young maiden was even more confused at what was unfolding before her. Then the angel told her that the whole plan had been mapped out, and the Holy Spirit will overshadow her. She accepted the plan with a YES.

The angel also said that an older cousin was also with child; the girl rushed to see her relative. A short while later; she was standing before Elizabeth, who, to the girl's surprise, told her that "she was blessed among all women" and astounded her by asking, "How is it that the mother of my Lord should come to visit me?"

Saint Luke the Evangelist reveals the identity of this virgin, writing: "The name of the virgin is Mary." She glorified God, who has done great things for her, and she noted, "From now, every generation shall call me blessed." She gave birth to and nurtured Jesus Christ, and after His death served as the mother of His Church, His spiritual body. At the end of her mortal life, she was assumed body and soul, into heaven.

Today, we still call her blessed because her role was ordained from the beginning of time. This book reflects on the biblical activities of the mother of God—our mother—and also her apparitions here on earth after her assumption into heaven.

In 1858 she appeared to a young French girl, Bernadette, and told her, "I am the Immaculate Conception." In 1917, she appeared to three shepherd children in Fatima, Portugal, and told them, "I come from heaven." She is our mother who art in heaven.

The Blessed Virgin Mary has played a role in our salvation since the beginning of time. She is a historical figure, and many books have been written about her. It is a known fact that not all Christians accord Mary the honor she is due. This book is a personal reflection, based on my devotion to the Blessed Mother and my conviction that she not only is the mother of God but our mother as well.

This book is based primarily on the biblical stories of the Blessed Virgin Mary and her apparitions; it reflects on the mother of God who is also our mother. The title of the book, *Our Mother Who Art in Heaven*, is derived from her personal statement to the three shepherd children in Fatima.

"I come from heaven," she told them when questioned by Lucia, the oldest of the three, about her mission and where she came from.

The first chapter discusses the creation of man, how man lost his glory, and his need for salvation. God promised to redeem man, so chapter 2 discusses the woman God chose to bear the Son of God who would redeem the fallen world. Since humanity had been condemned because of its disobedience, everybody was under original sin. A woman who bore the Son of God had to be specially prepared, so chapter 3 discusses the Immaculate Conception. Chapter 4 discusses the perpetual virginity of the Blessed Virgin Mary. Many non-Catholics believe that Mary had other children after the birth of Christ and, as such, could not be said to be an ever-virgin. Chapter 5 discusses Mary as the new Eve, the mother of the new people of God. The old Eve, like her husband, Adam, disobeyed God, but Mary, the new Eve, obeyed God, which led to the birth of the new people of God.

At the annunciation, the angel told Mary that she was going to be the mother of the Messiah and that her cousin

Elizabeth was also carrying a child, and Mary went to visit her. Chapter 6 describes Mary's visit to Elizabeth, where Elizabeth praised Mary and called her the mother of her Lord and the most blessed of all women. As chapter 7 explains, Mary then recited an inspired poem in praise of the God of Israel, who sent an angel to visit her despite of her lowly state, and future generations would call her blessed. Chapter 8 discusses the birth of Mary's son, Jesus Christ. Mary and Joseph, in keeping with the religious tradition of their people, presented the child in the temple, as demanded by the Mosaic law, this is covered in chapter 9.

The infant Jesus was threatened by King Herod, who saw Him as a threat; an angel told Joseph in a dream to take the child and flee to Egypt, which forms the basis of chapter 10. When Jesus was twelve, His parents took Him to the temple on their annual pilgrimage to Jerusalem. They finished everything they needed to do, but Jesus, without His parents' knowledge, stayed behind in the temple to do what He referred to as His "Father's business." Joseph and Mary's search for their son and their discovery of the child in the temple is discussed in chapter 11. Chapter 12 discusses Mary as the mother of God and our mother as well.

Chapter 13, "Our Mother Who Art in Heaven," discusses the different apparitions of the Blessed Virgin Mary, including the visions of Bernadette and the children in Fatima. Mary was not just a mother; she was a teacher who showed us how to receive gifts from God. We see this in her instruction to the stewards at the wedding feast in Cana, which is described in chapter 14. The final chapter discusses an accusation made by many Protestants against the Catholic Church, i.e., that Catholics worship Mary. Chapter 15 shows that Catholics do not worship Mary; the only being we worship is God. We do *honor* Mary, because God honored her to be the Mother of Christ, and the angel who brought the news said she was full of grace.

There are many publications on the Blessed Mother. I am only adding my little contribution. I hope more people will write and encourage devotion to the Blessed Mother and give her the honor she deserves.

1

The Creation and the Fall

"In the beginning," the Holy Book tells us, "God created the heavens and the earth, the earth was a formless wasteland, and darkness covered the abyss while a mighty wind swept over the waters" (Genesis1:1–2). This book of Genesis explains that God created everything and kept them in their proper places. He made a decision to create man: "Then God said, 'Let us make man in our image, after our likeness'"(Genesis 1:26). God obviously had a very clear picture of people before He created them. At creation, man was clean, pure, and innocent, just as God the creator desired him to be; he was made in the image and likeness of God Himself. God gave him authority over everything. He had created: plants, animals, birds, and the fish in the sea, which the Bible says were created in "their own kind." They were not created in the image of God, and so people were superior to them. Animals, birds, and all other creatures were made in a very simple way; God did not mold them as He did Adam. He simply made them by a divine fiat: "Let there be," and they came to be. Humans, as superior beings, had to be made by a creative act, and the Holy Scripture captures that historic moment:

> The Lord God formed man out of the clay
> of the ground and blew into his nostrils the
> breath of life, and so man became a living
> being. (Genesis 2:7)

There you have it: "the clay of the ground" and God's "breath of life" created living beings who were endowed with wisdom. As the only rational creatures in the world, humans had the privilege of talking with God as children talk to their father. Sometimes God came down and walked around the garden with them. It was a glorious moment for them, who had nothing to fear and enjoyed moving around the garden, admiring other creatures that God had created and given them authority over. It was a privilege that would have lasted a lifetime. The book of Genesis tells us how God used to stroll in the garden in the evening. I try to imagine such a sight: God walking around and smiling at Adam as they exchanged pleasantries. Man was truly in paradise. Everything God created was good. There were no electronic gadgets, no high-speed Internet, and yet our first parents enjoyed life to the fullest. This was because God was their source of happiness. It is a lesson for modern men and women who think that life consists of possessions. They walked around and played with animals and birds in the garden, and no one was hurt or attacked because of the mutual harmony that existed among them. There was a perfect unity and peace among the created things of this universe, something a modern mind finds it difficult to imagine. It was such a glorious moment for humanity, the devil became jealous.

Humans were the first to be created, but they had the singular privilege of being created in the image and likeness of God. They had a very cordial relationship with God until the devil entered the picture. The devil tempted them, who were a special creatures of God, and unfortunately they fell and were separated from God. They no longer enjoyed the comfort of His presence as they once did. After they disobeyed God, the relationship was no longer what it used to be; They were now afraid of God due to their guilty consciences. The book of Genesis records their first encounter with God after they disobeyed Him:

> When they heard the sound of the Lord
> God moving about in the garden at the
> breezy time of the day, the man and his wife
> hid themselves from the Lord God among
> the trees in the garden. (Genesis 3:8)

The presence of God scared them because of their guilt. They had been ambitious, they wanted to be like God, and for this illicit ambition, they had made the biggest mistake of their lives, i.e., they listened to the devil. They lost paradise. God sent them out of the Garden of Eden. They had been close to God's heart when they listened to Him, but they were out roaming in an uncultivated land and with a curse on their heads. The evil one who deceived them, now out of sight, was happy that they had lost their good relationship with God.

Darkness fell upon the earth because the light of God, which had always led the people, was extinguished by their inordinate thirst for knowledge. God loved them and gave them everything; He made them rule over other creatures, who were subject to man and woman. They lacked nothing, but they were greedy and wanted to be like the One who created them—just because the evil one put that idea into the woman's head. That is the case even today: we always want more and are never satisfied with what we have.

God used to walk with them in the garden, but He no longer showed up. Adam and Eve were forced to confront the consequences of their disobedience. Once friendly animals and birds became hostile to one another, and some became wild and dangerous to humans. The earth that was once a very peaceful habitat became a place characterized by the survival of the fittest. Evil, sickness, and death entered the world. This was exactly what the devil wanted, because he was threatened by the cordial relationship that existed between God and humans. The devil would have lost his place in the world if people were totally obedient to God. The devil wanted disciples he could use to oppose God and perpetuate evil in the world. He is happy and takes credit when people sin against God. By obeying the devil and disobeying God, people alienated themselves from God and were condemned to roam the earth without Him.

However, God still cared about humanity. Generations later, He would use a strong hand to remove His chosen people from the pharaoh in Egypt, but He no longer dwelled with them as He once did in the garden, because of their obstinacy. Moses, the chosen leader of the people, prayed and entreated the Lord to dwell with them once again, but He would not. God said that if He were to live among them, He would have exterminated them, because people refused to acknowledge His authority and often rebelled against

Him. Moses told this to the people. This is how the book of Exodus reports it.

> The Lord said to Moses, "Tell the Israelites:
> you are a stiff-necked people. Were I to go
> up in your company even for a moment, I
> would exterminate you. (Exodus 33:5)

However, the Lord did not totally walk away from the people. He decided to dwell in the Ark of the Covenant, which was positioned in the Holy of Holies in the temple, where only the high priest was allowed to enter. The people were not holy enough for the Lord to dwell with them. The question was, would there ever be a way out? What would happen to the people? Would they ever return to the garden and dwell with God? When would this be resolved? A statement by psalmist describes the situation well: "Now we see no signs, we have no prophets, no one knows how long" (Psalm 74:9). In addition, Micah's prophecy gave a clue about what would happen and when to future generations. He prophesied about a woman who would give birth; until then the Lord will allow people to be on their own.

> Therefore the Lord will give them up, until
> the time when she who is to give birth has
> borne."(Micah 5:2)

She who is to give birth. According to Saint Jerome, Micah was referring to the messianic mother: "in the name of the Lord, the king shall shepherd his flock." This verse refers to the role of the Virgin promised by the prophets. It refers to the role the Blessed Virgin Mary would play in the history of salvation, which would take place at the appointed time. As Saint Paul writes:

> But when the fullness of time had come, God sent His Son, born of a woman, born under the law, to ransom those under the law, so that we might receive adoption. As proof that you are children, God sent the spirit of His Son into our hearts, crying out "Abba Father!" so you are no longer a slave but a child … (Galatians 4:4–7)

By this, the slaves became freeborn. Man was restored to his position once again.

With Mary, the salvation of humanity was set in motion. Her "yes" to God liberated humanity. The lost state of man was restored by the birth of Christ, as Saint Paul mentions above. In the words of Fulton Sheen:

> The image of man that was first ruined in the revolt against God in Eden was restored when the woman brought forth a Man—a perfect man without sin, but a man personally united with God. He is the pattern of the new race of men, who would be called Christians.[1]

There was a plan in the pipeline. While the fall of Adam and Eve was a sad thing in human history, the redemption

---

[1] Fulton J. Sheen, *The World's First Love: Mary, Mother of God* (San Francisco: Ignatius Press, 2015), p. 105.

remains the most joyful and benevolent event in the history of mankind. It showcased the ultimate love of God, which culminated in His taking flesh and becoming like humans in all things but sin. It was a happy fall, as we sing at the Easter vigil liturgy. It was at that moment that God introduced a new woman to the public, a woman who was in His plan of salvation from the beginning of time. This woman was Mary. Pope Saint John Paul wrote, "The Mother of the Redeemer has a precise place in the plan of salvation."[2]

Mary, the mother of the Redeemer was not just an accident that happened on the road to the human salvation. She was part of God's plan. "Mary was in His plan from the very beginning," writes Scott Hahn, "chosen and foretold from the moment God created man and woman."[3]

So when the first woman disobeyed God by listening to the devil, a new woman was already in the pipeline, a woman who would listen to and obey God. When God created man and woman and put them in the garden of Eden, He gave them everything they needed to live a comfortable life. He also gave them freedom to choose. The devil did not allow people to enjoy this gift; he came around and deceived Adam and Eve into disobedience. God drove them out of the garden, cursing humanity and the earth as He did so. When God pronounced this curse on the serpent, He said, "I will put enmity between you and the woman, and between your offspring and hers", (Genesis 3:15). The serpent deceived the woman into eating the forbidden fruit, which brought

---

[2] John Paul II, *Redemptoris Mater* (March 25, 1987), p. 1.

[3] Scott Hahn, *Hail, Holy Queen: The Mother of God in the Word of God* (New York: Image Books,Doubleday, 2001), p. 32.

condemnation to the created world. In God's plan, it would be the seed of another woman who not only would stand up to the devil but would crush him These two created beings would play significant roles in the future of God's people. The woman and her offspring would constantly be in conflict with the devil and his offspring. Pope St. John Paul II places Mary at the center of the conflict: "Mary, the Mother of the Incarnate Word, is placed at the very center of that enmity, that struggle which accompanies the history of humanity on earth and the history of salvation itself."[4]

The devil does not feel happy when the children of God have a good relationship with their heavenly Father. Even after he caused havoc by severing the relationship between God and man, he kept on fighting. The fight is so severe that Saint Peter warned the children of God in very strong words: "Be sober and vigilant. Your opponent the devil is prowling around like a roaring lion looking for someone to devour" (1 Peter 5:8). The devil sees those who obey God as his opponents and he goes after them. He continues to fight the seed of the woman. The woman reappears in Revelation 12, where John describes a woman who is about to give birth:

> A great sign appeared in the sky, a woman clothed with the sun, with a moon under her feet, and on her head a crown of twelve stars. She was with child … then another sign appeared in the sky; it was a huge dragon … Then the dragon stood before the woman about to give birth, to devour

---

[4] John Paul II, *Redemptoris Mater*, 11.

her child when she gave birth. (Revelation
12:1–4)

This time the dragon did not succeed, as it had in the book
of Genesis when it deceived the woman. This passage is
primarily interpreted to refer to the church, but the church
is the offspring of the woman.

God promised His people that they would not be doomed
forever: "The days are coming, says the Lord, when I will
make a new covenant with the house of Israel and the house
of Judah" (Jeremiah 31:31). God told them, "I will give
you a new heart and place a new Spirit within you, taking
from your bodies your stony hearts and giving you natural
hearts" (Ezekiel 36:26). One particular person would carry
out this act of renewal, the Messiah, birthed by a virgin at
the proper time.

The people of God waited in hope for the fulfillment of
the promise God made to their forefathers. Through the
mouths of the prophets, God had promised the people a
new relationship. God would decide when this would be
fulfilled. He had put everything in place, waiting for the
time of redemption, but it would not be easy as it would
entail the shedding of His Son's blood. He took on human
flesh and was born of a virgin at the appointed time. He
lined up a number of Old Testament figures and prophets to
inform the people about His arrival and that of the one who
would point Him out to the world when He finally arrived:
"Behold the Lamb of God," he would say, using a title
reserved only for the Messiah. Since God is the architect of
time, He knows how to control it and use it for the purposes
He deems fit. His Son would come at the appointed time,

but the maiden, who would bring Him to the world, would have to be prepared and set aside. The prophet who foretold of the coming simply said "a virgin" and did not mention who she would be. It was a long time before the prophecy was fulfilled, as Saint Paul says, "at the appointed time," when the Virgin who had been prepared from the beginning of time would be revealed. She would bear the Son of God, whose mission would be to bring salvation to the people who waited in hope for His coming, the Word that in the beginning was with God, who would take on human flesh and dwell among humans. For this to occur, He had to take His flesh and blood from a human like us, which would make Him fully human and fully God. The role of the Virgin that was prophesied within the salvation history was pointed out by the council fathers:

> The Sacred Scriptures of both the Old and the New Testament, as well as ancient Tradition show the role of the Mother of the Savior in the economy of salvation in an ever clearer light and draw attention to it. The books of the Old Testament describe the history of salvation, by which the coming of Christ into the world was slowly prepared.[5]

---

[5] *Lumen Gentium* (November 21, 1964), n. 55.

2

She Who Was Chosen

> The world being unworthy to receive
> the Son of God directly from the hands
> of the Father, He gave His Son to Mary
> for the world to receive Him from her.
> —Saint Augustine

For the Son of God to come to the world, He had to come through a channel, a woman who would give birth to Him. A special woman was needed. She had been in God's mind at creation; she was in the Word of God. Her presence in the scriptures and the special action of God at her birth make her the highly favored one, who is full of grace. God knew her before she was born. By the special grace of God, she became one of the actors in the divine drama of human salvation. The Savior of mankind, who existed before time began, became flesh in her womb; thus, she was the chosen one. The Word became flesh in the womb of a woman. This was an unprecedented event in human history. It pointed to the uniqueness of God. He is a God of possibilities. He brought forth human salvation in a very special way: God became man.

The salvation of man was something unique; nothing of this nature had ever happened before. Man who was created to know God, love Him, and serve Him, to be with Him in eternity, had disobeyed Him and earned damnation. But the benevolent God later reversed the punishment and promised to redeem man. It was in God's mind from the beginning of time to have a woman bear His Son. The holy prophets prophesied this in the early days of the people of God. The Messiah who will bring salvation was to be born of a maiden. The fact that the prophets spoke about her shows that she was already in God's mind and her identity was kept close to His heart. Only God knew who she was and that she would bear His Son. The people had expected a Messiah but were not too concerned about whom the maiden would be. All they wanted was a Messiah to deliver them from their sins. The world that had been in darkness, and the people walking in the shadow of death were waiting for the Messiah to come and deliver them. Therefore, whoever the Virgin was did not so much matter; salvation was the uppermost thing in their minds. There were many young maidens in the region, but nobody knew which one would be the chosen Virgin. God knew about her because He had prepared her before she was born and assigned her the onerous task of bringing forth the Savior of the world. All this was already in God's blueprint for the world's salvation.

Did she know she would be the mother of God? It does not seem so, judging from her reaction to the angel. She was shocked when the angel came to announce the coming of Christ and God's plan for her. Like all Jewish people of the day, she knew that a Messiah was coming, but she did not know she would bring Him forth. So when the angel described her role in God's plan for human salvation, she asked, "How can this be, since I know no man?"

She had to be prepared in a very special way, for she would give flesh and blood to the Son of God. Neither her parents nor the one to whom she was betrothed, Joseph, were party to this plan. They, like Mary, had to embrace it, because it was God's will. The parents did not know that their child would bear the Son of God, so they did not prepare her for this task. Of course, no one could do that since it was something unprecedented and very unique. Nobody had ever given birth to God before; therefore, no one knew what techniques—for giving birth to and nursing God—were required. As the angel told Mary at the annunciation, "The Holy Spirit will overshadow you." One of the jobs of the Holy Spirit was to direct her on how to be the mother of God. Later, Jesus described the Holy Spirit to His apostles: "The Advocate, the Holy Spirit that the Father will send in my name, He will teach you everything …" (John 14: 26). The Spirit was already present to teach Mary her role as the mother of God. God therefore prepared her personally from the moment of her conception—not just to be the mother of God but to understand the teachings of the Holy Spirit. She would be the new Ark of the Covenant who would carry the word of God in the flesh as the new Eve—the mother of those who have new life in Christ.

God does His things His own way. He does not need the approval of humans or follow human logic to do His work. He consults no one because His ways are different from ours. This can be clearly seen in the words which He spoke through the mouth of prophet Isaiah:

> For my thoughts are not your thoughts,
> nor are your ways my ways … As high as
> the heavens are above the earth, so high are
> my ways above your ways and my thoughts
> above your thoughts. (Isaiah 55:8–9)

Saint Paul asked, "For who has known the mind of the Lord or who has been His counselor?" (Romans 11:34). God's actions sometimes besmirch human logic. People who only rely on human logic to understand the workings of God, are bound to make mistake in their belief, a mistake that can be attributed to crass ignorance. God chose Mary and made her sinless from birth, what we know in Catholic teaching as the Immaculate Conception. To further strengthen this presentation, I want to take some time here to look at the Immaculate Conception of the Blessed Virgin Mary. It pleased God from the first moment to make her holy. Chosen by God from the beginning, she remains the ever-virgin mother of Christ.

3

Conceived Immaculate

To understand the Immaculate Conception of the Blessed Virgin Mary, let us look at her as the vessel that was designed to convey the word of God, i.e., the Son of God. She was the New Testament version of the Ark of the Covenant. One very interesting thing that we notice in the history of our salvation is the duplication of events, images, and people in the Old and New Testaments. Many of the things that happened in the Old Testament prefigured the things we see in the New Testament. One of them is, the Ark of the Covenant, which the Blessed Virgin Mary came to represent.

The Ark of the Covenant was the most sacred artifact in the Old Testament It was kept in the Temple in the Holy of Holies, out of bounds to everybody except the high priest, who only entered the sanctuary a few times a year. The Ark of the Covenant was holy because it contained sacred objects. Scott Hahn describes it this way:

The dogma of the mmaculate onception was promulgated by Pope Pius IX. In the onstitution *Ineffabilis Deus* (December 8, 1854), he stated that the "Most Blessed Virgin Mary, in the first instance of her conception, by a singular privilege and grace granted by God, in view of the merits of Jesus Christ the Savior of the human race, was preserved free from all stain of original sin." It is through this special grace and sanctity of life that she was able to stand victorious over the ancient serpent, the enemy of the human race. Freed from the ancient curse upon the human race, she would bear the Son of God, who would free His people from sin and rule over the house of David forever. Given all we know about the Blessed Virgin Mary, we can say, therefore, that it was not flesh and blood that inspired Elizabeth to call her "blessed among women," it was the prompting of the Holy Spirit. No other human on earth merited such grace. She was honored by God; therefore, we are obliged to honor her as well. No wonder Mary said He that is mighty had done great things for her. God singled her out and granted her the grace of sanctification to be a dwelling place for His Son. Archbishop Fulton Sheen said of her immaculate conception, "She was redeemed in advance, by way of prevention, in both body and soul, in the first instant of conception."[7]

The belief that the Blessed Virgin Mary, the mother of the Son of God, was born stained with the original sin—like any of us—disrespects the wisdom and authority of God. Scott Hahn quotes Saint Augustine as saying that it would be an offense against Jesus to say that His mother was a sinner.[8] That happens to be precisely what those who deny

---

[7] Sheen, *The World's First Love*, p. 8.

[8] Hahn, *Hail, Holy Queen*, p. 96.

the immaculate conception say. I am not being judgmental here; I'm only stating a fact.

God, it should be noted, can clean up anyone to carry out His mission. It would be sacrilege to say that the Son of God, who is holy, could be formed in the womb and take the flesh of a human tainted by sin generated by the fall of humanity.

Anyone who is still in doubt should look at the call of the prophet Isaiah, a human being assigned a mission by God. Isaiah acknowledged that God had to clean him up before he could carry out his mission. In a vision, he was presented before the throne of God. The scene was so terrifying that he called out:

> Then I said, "Woe is me, I am doomed!
> For I am a man of unclean lips; yet my
> eyes have seen the King, the Lord of host!"
> Then one of the Seraphim flew to me,
> holding an ember which he had taken with
> the tongs from the altar. He touched my
> mouth with it.
> "See," he said, "now this has touched your
> lips, your wickedness is removed, your sin
> is purged." (Isaiah 6:5–7)

If God could cleanse the person who delivered His message to His people, how much more would He do for His Son's own mother, who would carry Him in her womb and share her flesh and blood with Him? The dogma of the mmaculate onception does not need much of a theological explanation. It just requires common sense and a mind that is open to the truth. But many people are closed to the truth of the gospel.

Some people are just biased and block their minds, because the truth can derail their own misleading teachings. Some people argue against the Immaculate Conception because, according to them, Mary was a human being who needed redemption. My question is, redemption by whom? If Jesus is the redeemer of the human race, would it be difficult for Him to wave off the impediment and redeem Mary first, making her an immaculate and perfect dwelling place for Him? To refuse to believe that insults the power of the omnipotent God. Why do people continue to deny that the Blessed Mother was born immaculate? By refusing to believe, these people are trying to limit God by defining Him in human terms. They don't accept that He can do extraordinary things. He who created the world ex nihilo and made man sinless before the fall also could single out a soul and make her immaculate so she could carry His Son and bring Him into the world.

During her apparition at Lourdes, the Blessed Virgin Mary introduced herself as the mmaculate onception. She told this to Bernadette Soubirous, whom she visited for several months in 1858. She promised to reveal herself to the girl and in the last month of her visit, she said: "I am the Immaculate Conception." Her testimony is true because she is credible. A woman who bore the Son of God should be trusted. We have no reason to doubt Blessed Mary. She is not a liar. She is not a politician, who always claims to be something else to get votes from the people. From the moment of her conception, she has been free from original sin. If the church had made any mistake in the dogma of mmaculate onception, she would have corrected when she introduced herself to Bernadette. Instead, she confirmed that she is truly the Immaculate Conception. The fathers at the second Vatican Council had every reason to believe this, stating:

> Adorned from the first instant of her conception with the radiance of an entirely unique holiness, the Virgin of Nazareth is greeted, on God's command, By an angel messenger as "full of grace."[9]

Once again, this proves she was sinless from birth. Truly, the argument that she is free from original sin should not pose any difficulty for anyone who knows God's modus operandi. If He created the world from nothing, what would then prevent Him from creating a human being as a channel to bring His sinless Son into the world? The problem is that we look at everything from a human angle and subject everything to a logical formula. When John the Baptist told the people, "For I tell you, God can raise up children to Abraham from these stones"(Luke 3:8), he was hinting that God can do anything He wants, even produce life from inanimate objects. Considering the omnipotence of God and all that God has done from the moment of creation,to create Mary free from original sin would not be difficult for Him. To say otherwise is to limit the power of God. Would the God who is holy place His Son in a womb tainted with original sin when He could cleanse that womb and make it a fit place for His Word made flesh? Common sense tells us the opposite is true. God had the power to make a perfect place for His Son.

---

[9] *Lumen Gentium*, 56.

Those who still see the Blessed Mary as just another human are simply saying that Jesus took a flesh from a sinful human being. Mary was sinless from the moment of her conception so that, as the angel said at the annunciation, "The child to be born will be called holy, the Son of God" (Luke 1:35). If the angel was not afraid to call her blessed, who are we to do otherwise?

The Presentation

Father Don Miller OFM, citing the *Protoevangelium of James*, tells us that Anna and Joachim offered Mary to God in the temple when she was three years old. They did this to carry out the promise they had made to God when they were childless. Anna had promised to dedicate her child to God. Little did she know God's plan for her child, who was chosen, even before she was born, to bear the Savior of mankind. The presentation of Mary signaled her perpetual vocation of living for God. Without the knowledge of anybody except her parents, Mary was given to God to spend her life in His service. That is probably why she called herself the handmaid of the Lord when the angel brought the news to her. This means she already knew she had been dedicated and so belonged to God, although she did not know she would give birth to the Son of God. She professed to be a handmaid to her Son, the God who would become flesh and dwell among His people.

The presentation of a child by the parents in the temple was not a strange practice in ancient times. The book of Samuel tells us that Hannah presented her son, Samuel, to the Lord as she had promised.

4

Forever a Virgin

According to Jewish tradition, there were some young maidens known as temple virgins, whose primary duties were to take care of the temple. They kept it clean, sewed liturgical garments, and decorated the temple. They remained in the temple until they reached the marriageable age of fourteen, when they would be discharged. Some were taken into the temple very early in their lives. They were under the supervision and tutelage of older women, mostly widows who were still active after the loss of their husbands. Anna the prophetess—who the scriptures tell us went into the temple when Jesus was presented there—was one of those widows. The Blessed Virgin Mary was one of the temple virgins. According to Anne Catherine Emmerich:

> The Blessed Virgin lived with other virgins in the temple under the care of pious matrons. The maidens employed themselves with embroidery and other forms of decoration of carpets and vestments, and

> also with the cleaning of these vestments
> and of the vessels used in the temple.[10]

In a vision, Emmerich was shown an aspect of the life of the Blessed Virgin Mary that was not known to others. Mary had made a vow of perpetual virginity to God while she served as a temple virgin. This meant that she would not have relations with a man. Some people argue against the idea that she was perpetual virgin because, according to them, there is no evidence for it in any secular writings outside the Catholic circle. There is a strong evidence of her perpetual virginity embedded in the dialogue at the annunciation. When the angel appeared to Mary, she was already betrothed to Joseph. Why didn't they have relations? It would have been perfectly okay, as they were married. Certainly they had no idea as yet that God had planned to make Mary the mother of His incarnate Son. Thus, there was no reason other than that Mary had taken a vow of perpetual virginity and Joseph may have found this out when the angel revealed her true betrothed, and he clearly understood.

Telling a married woman she will conceive and bear a son is stating the obvious, since reproduction is a biological necessity. The woman would not have any reason to doubt the statement since procreation is an aspect of marriage. But if the woman had doubts and asked, "How can this be since I have not had relations with a man?" that might mean she did not recognize the man as her husband or that they did not intend to have relations. Mary's question to the angel confirms that she'd vowed never to have a relations with a

---

[10] Anne Emmerich, *TheLife of the Blessed Virgin Mary* (Charlotte, NC: TAN Books, 2011), p. 129.

man. As Saint Augustine said, "Had she intended to know man, she would not have been amazed. Her amazement is a sign of vow."[11] This confirms that Mary was a perpetual virgin. When she appeared to Juan Diego in Guadalupe on December 9, 1531, she introduced herself this way: "My dear little son, I love you. I desire you to know who I am. I am the ever-virgin Mary, Mother of the ever true God who gives life and maintains its existence."

Another statement from our Blessed Mother confirms her perpetual virginity. On November 29, 1932, in Beauraing, Belgium, our Lady appeared to some young children, ages nine to fifteen. She introduced herself as the "Immaculate Virgin." She asked the children, "Do you love my Son? Do you love me?" She urged the children to "pray, pray, pray." And, as she did in many other places, she directed a chapel to be built in the spot. She would not have introduced herself as the mmaculate irgin if she'd had other children besides Jesus and had lost her virginity, as some people want us to believe. To maintain that the Blessed Virgin Mary lost her virginity after the birth of Christ, in my opinion, is unfair to the mother of God, who dedicated her life to holy service by giving birth to and raising the Son of God.

Since the Creator put a curse on earth because of the fall of Adam and Eve, God was alienated from His creatures. Adam and Eve were sent out of the Garden of Eden. God, being a merciful Father, did not abandon people to eternal suffering but promised a Messiah.

---

[11] Tim Stapples, *Behold Your Mother: Biblical and Historical Defense of the Marian Doctrines* (El Cajon, CA: Catholic Answers, Inc., 2014), p. 132.

Isaiah prophesied that there was hope for the people who were sitting in darkness, awaiting their redemption. The messianic prophet said a Messiah would come via a woman. A virgin, Isaiah said, shall conceive and bear a son and shall call Him Immanuel, which means "God is with us." While the people waited, a young Jewish girl grew up in a poor neighborhood in the little village of Nazareth, ignorant about what she would be saddled with.

Paul pointed out that at the appointed time God's Son was born of a woman. This woman had been on God's God from the beginning of time and was revealed when the angel Gabriel announced that she had been chosen to bear the Savior. Her name was Mary.

She was not born to royalty, but she grew up to become a queen. Her parents, Joachim and Anne, were not elite members of the community, and so her childhood was uncelebrated; she was just like any other young girl in her neighborhood. One thing is certain: she was devoted to her religious duties. She spent a fair amount of time in prayer. She consecrated her life to God, not because she expected to bear the Son of God but because it was her duty. Many of the people who came in contact with her saw her as an ordinary Jewish girl. Even Joseph, her betrothed, did not have the slightest idea who she was. Here is what Tim Stapples says in support of the perpetual virginity of the Blessed Virgin Mary:

> According to Scripture and ancient Jewish tradition, Mary belonged to the father of her child—the Holy Spirit. However the Holy Spirit could not be the protector that

Mary needed. The Holy Spirit could not
sign legal documents and be Mary's legal
spouse. But Joseph was ready and willing—
just man that he was—to care for Mary as
his lawfully wedded wife.[12]

Joseph could not have had relations with Mary as long as
she was carrying someone else's child. By tradition, Mary
rightfully belonged to the father of her child, which is why
she often is referred to as the "spouse of the Holy Spirit."
It would not have been possible for Mary to have another
child after Jesus, since His coming was planned, and the
Holy Spirit became her spiritual spouse.

The Guest from Heaven

As a very devout Jewish maiden, Mary either must have
read or been told about the Old Testament scriptures. She

---

[12] Stapples, *Behold Your Mother*, pp.150–51.

must have come across or heard about angels appearing to the patriarchs, but she probably never saw an angel in real life. One can imagine her shock when this heavenly figure was not just standing before her but greeting her with a heavenly salutation, "Hail, full of grace, the Lord is with you" (Luke 1:28).

She must have held her breath in fear and tried to wish away the scene. Her adrenalin must have shot higher than normal. She must have wondered what was happening and if she would survive the episode. She had to be petrified, until the lovely figure before her said, "Do not be afraid Mary, for you have found favor with God." Then the angel slowly unfolded the divine plan of salvation for humanity in which she had been chosen to participate. "You shall conceive and bear a Son …" the angel told her.

At this point, she was more relaxed but still could not totally understand the scene unfolding before her. Knowing that this was the will of God gave her courage. She found her voice and asked the angel, "How can this be since I know no man?" Mary was concerned about her vowed virginity. Would she have to break her vow to God to bring forth the Son of God?

The angel told her the process; "The Holy Spirit will come upon you, and the power of the Most High will overshadow you. Therefore the one to be born will be called the Son of the Most High." By mentioning the Holy Spirit, the angel calmed her nerves, even though the Holy Spirit was not often seen. The Old Testament people knew about the Spirit of Yahweh, so it was not difficult for Mary to recognize that the angel meant the divine person of the Godhead.

The process was not ordinary. She was then convinced that this mission would not in any way violate her vow to God to remain a perpetual virgin. She saw in this mission another way to fulfill her vow and said to the angel, "I am the handmaid of the Lord; let it be done to me according to thy word." With this statement, she surrendered herself to God so that His plan would be fulfilled, leading to the salvation of humanity and the emergence of a new people. Pope Paul VI in his apostolic exhortation of May 13, 1967, commented on this moment of Mary's consent:

> From that moment, she consecrated all of herself to the service not only of the heavenly Father and of the Word Incarnate, who had become her Son, but also to all mankind, having clearly understood that Jesus, in addition to saving His people from slavery of sin, would become the king of a messianic kingdom, universal and eternal.[13]

In the same vein, Pope Saint John Paul pointed out that Mary's agreement to bear the Son of God gave rise to a new people of God: "In the salvific economy of God's revelation Abraham's faith constitutes the beginning of the Old Covenant; Mary's faith at the Annunciation inaugurates the New covenant."[14]

After the angel had departed, Mary must have spent quite some time pondering this thing in her heart. She was not sure what had happened to her, but her perfect trust and

---

[13] Paul VI, *Signum Magnum*, pt. 1.

[14] John Paul II, *Redemptoris Mater*, 14.

faith in God allowed her to accept the Word because, in the long run, it would be for the good of the people. From the moment Mary said yes she gave up her personal goals and joined God's plan for the salvation of humanity. Everything from that point would be done according to God's plan.

In her innocence, she had protested, as many people in the Old Testament—Moses, Jeremiah, and some of the prophets—had done, but when the angel told her it was the will of God, she accepted with a yes. At that moment, the "Word became flesh" in the womb of the Virgin. Her yes was the beginning of the pilgrimage of faith, which would end in the eternal kingdom, for she bore the One who would gather the children of men around the divine Father. The prophecy was fulfilled when Mary became the mother of the One who would redeem the world, as the angel told Joseph in a dream. She became the divine channel through which the Savior came into the world. Her role in the salvation history began when she responded with a yes to the proposal presented to her by the angel Gabriel. She became the first human being to participate in the plan of God. The prophets were only God's mouthpieces, foretelling the salvation to come, but she was an active participant. She accepted and acted immediately to execute the first item on the agenda.

The annunciation was successful at least in two ways: (1) the Redeemer of the world was conceived in the womb of the Virgin of Nazareth, and (2) humanity gained a new life from a new Eve, the new mother of all the living. Her readiness to do God's will introduced something new to the relationship between God and man. It ended the alienation and created a new world for humanity. Bishop Barron described Mary's humble acceptance in this way:

> And in obediently adding, "may it be done to me according to your word," she reversed the grasping disobedience of Eve. This is why the medieval illustrators and commentatorso in love with the parallels, rhymes, and echoes within the Bible— imagined the Ave ("hail") of the angel reversing Eva (Eve).[15]

---

[15] Robert Barron, *Catholicism* (New York: Image Books, 2011), p. 91.

5

Mary as the New Eve

> The Father of mercies willed that the
> incarnation should be preceded by the
> acceptance of her who was predestined to
> be the mother of His Son, so that just as
> a woman contributed to death, so also a
> woman should contribute to life.[16]

Mary surrendered herself to the Will of God, saying, "I
am the handmaid of the Lord. Be it done to me according
to thy Word." With these words, the maiden of Nazareth
heralded a new beginning. The Word was made flesh in her
womb. The curse incurred by Adam and Eve soon would be
reversed. A new generation of God's children would be born
when Mary brought forth God in the flesh. The Lord God
had promised His people, through the mouth of prophet
Ezekiel, "I will open your graves and have you rise from
them ... Then you shall know that I am the Lord, when I
open your graves and have you rise from them, O my people.
I will put my spirit in you that you may live, ... thus you

---

[16] *Lumen Gentium*, 56.

shall know that I am the Lord. I have promised, and I will do it ..." (Ezekiel 37:12–14). The Lord also said, "You shall be my people, and I will be your God" (Jeremiah 30:22). And the prophet Jeremiah announced, "The Lord has created a new thing upon earth: the woman must encompass the man with devotion" (Jeremiah 31:22).

"A new thing on earth" is a reference to the role of the new woman, who now represents faith in God's Word. According to Scott Hahn, the woman in the book of the Apocalypse is the same woman in the old covenant, that is, Eve.

> Tradition tells us that she is the same person whom Jesus calls "woman" in John's gospel, the reprise of the person Adam calls "woman" in the Garden of Eden. Like the beginning of John's gospel, this episode of the Apocalypse repeatedly evokes the *Protoevangelium* of Genesis.[17]

Perhaps the reason Jesus always addresses His mother as "woman" in scripture is to point out, as Hahn suggests above, that Mary is not just His mother but the woman at the beginning of human existence.

People call Mary the new Eve because she brought life into the world that was dead. She is the mother of the new life, the mother of the living. She is the mother of a new generation of God's people. Eve, in the old dispensation, wanted to be like God, to know everything God knew, and

---

[17] Hahn, *Hail, Holy Queen*, p. 59

thought she could achieve this by listening to and believing the devil. Mary humbled herself before God by listening and believing the angel from heaven. She opened herself up to the Will of God and made herself available for Him to use for the good of humanity. According to Bishop Barron, "In this [way,] she becomes the Eve, the mother of all those who would be reborn by being receptive to God's life as a gift."[18]

Unlike the old Eve, Mary submitted herself to God; the Will of God took precedence in her life. Once Mary accepted, the salvation plan could kick off. God's age-long promise to His people was set to roll. With the cooperation of the Holy Spirit, the Word became flesh, and God soon smiled again with humanity.

Mary became the new Eve who brought about the new creation. After the fall, God cursed the earth, and nothing good could come from it. Through the incarnation of His Son, Mary became the mother of God's new people. The fruit of her womb brought forth a new creation. Saint Paul said, "So whoever is in Christ is a new creation: the old things have passed away; behold, new things have come" (2 Corinthians 5:17).

God's new people, therefore, began with Mary. The old creatures that came from Eve had been condemned, and God started writing on a new slate when Mary surrendered to God's Will and became the mother of His Son. In turn, Jesus would bring forth a new generation of the people of God. Mary started a new era in Jesus Christ. Saint John said, "All things came to be through Him and without Him

---

[18] Barron, *Catholicism*, p. 91

nothing came to be. What came to be through Him was life and this life was the light of the human race; the light shines in the darkness and the darkness has not overcome it" (John 1:3–5). Saint Paul called Jesus the image of the invisible God; in his letter to the Colossians he referred to Him as the "firstborn of all creation"(1 Colossians 1:15). To be a firstborn, one has to be born. If Jesus was the firstborn, then obviously the person who gave birth to Him has to be the first mother of created things.

The marriage feast at Cana, as recorded by John, is a very beautiful scene that points to Mary as this new Eve. On behalf of the wedding hosts, she asked her Son for a favor, which He initially rejected but later obliged. Thus He who came to do the Will of His Father—i.e., to fulfill the spiritual needs of the people of God—started by doing His mother's will to satisfy the physical needs of the people. When He said "woman," He was describing the "woman" in the book of Genesis. When He said "my hour has not yet come," He was talking about the "hour" when He would fulfill the Will of the Father. By performing this miracle at Cana, changing water into wine at the wedding, He demonstrated that something new had happened, a new generation has begun. Unlike Eve led the old Adam to disobey God, Mary led the new Adam to do the Will of the Father.

Mary's role in the salvation history can been seen all through the scriptures. Every moment of her earthly life was dedicated to this role, which had been set up for her by the Father. Her major role as the mother of the Redeemer was the beginning of this salvific ministry. Tim Stapples writes,

She continues in that prophetic role from the wedding Feast of Cana in John 2 to the foot of the Cross in John 19 and indeed until the end of time in Revelation 12, bringing life to all of her spiritual children "who keep the commandments of God and bear testimony to Jesus."[19]

---

[19] Stapples, *Behold Your Mother*, p. 97.

6

Mary Visits Elizabeth

The angel Gabriel delivered other important news to Mary: "And behold, Elizabeth, your relative, has also conceived a son in her old age, and this is the sixth month for her who was called barren" (Luke 1:36). When Mary received news, I can imagine that many things came into her mind, but the most important thing that occurred to her likely was Elizabeth's advanced age.

Pregnancy causes enough stress when you are young, let alone if you are at an age when you should be in a retirement home. One can only imagine what Elizabeth went through at that moment. Mary must have thought about this and probably imagined her aged cousin, with child, dragging herself across the kitchen floor, trying to fix dinner. Before the angel departed, however, he made a statement that dismissed her fears and became a philosophy for all believers: "for nothing will be impossible for God" (Luke 1:37). God demonstrated this frequently in the lives of the chosen people, and He showed it again by allowing someone who had passed child-bearing age to conceive a child. God controls time and aging.

The angel was not saying anything new; he was simply stating an obvious fact: God would intervene in the salvation history of the chosen people, which underscored His omnipotence. The events shaped by God made the chosen people the envy of other nations which included the dividing of the Red Sea, bringing forth water from the rock, raining manna from heaven in the desert. Now the virgin birth of His Son would complete the salvation plan. This was meant to prove that Elizabeth's pregnancy was part of the salvation plan, for she would give birth to the precursor of Christ.

Mary forgot that she was carrying the Son of God; she ran in haste to the hill country where her cousin resided. Given the urgency of the situation, I cannot imagine that she even had time to stop and inform her betrothed or her parents about this new development in her life. All she was concerned about was how to help this aged expectant mother.

Carrying the Son of the Father in her womb, she left in haste and headed to the hill country of Judea. It was a long walk, which should have been tedious for a first-time expectant mother, but she was able to accomplish it because she was filled with the zeal to do the will of God, and the Holy Spirit was upon her. At creation, the Spirit of the Lord had hovered over the water. Now the Spirit of God was chaperoning the maiden who would bring forth the Redeemer, who had been planned from the beginning of time.

After Mary's brief but effective encounter with the angel, everything changed. Not only did the destiny of humanity but also Mary's own plans for herself changed once she headed to Judea. There, she entered the house of Zachariah, and another dramatic scene in salvation history took place. Two women—with great disparity in their ages, both carrying babies whose different missions both aimed to liberate fallen humanity—stood face to face with one another. The old dispensation meets the new, and the babies in their wombs blend both.

When Mary arrived, something she did not expect happened. Elizabeth who came out to welcome her did not see the little cousin she knew but a living tabernacle, enclosing the precious baby King. She saw the ancient Ark of the Covenant bearing the word of God and the new law embodied in the flesh of the new King. Mary on her part did not see a frail and feeble grandmother-looking expectant mother but a figure from the old dispensation, energized by the Holy Spirit. Elizabeth's powerful voice confirmed that there was more inside her than what the naked eye could see. She was carrying the one who would announce the one Mary was carrying to the world. The meeting of these two women of grace generated a lot of text from which generations after generations would continue to learn.

When Mary entered the house, Elizabeth's strong voice must have startled her as did the strange things she said. She "cried out in a loud voice," which made Mary wonder where she got such strength. At her age, Elizabeth was supposed to be feeble with a weak voice. When Mary was walking that long distance to Judea, she expected to meet an elderly and frail woman. That was not to be; here is a clear manifestation that the work of God is everywhere. What Elizabeth said shocked Mary more: "Most blessed are you among women, and blessed is the fruit of your womb" (Luke 1:42).

Mary must have watched her in shock, as she'd watched the angel a short while before. She must have asked herself how Elizabeth managed to get the information Mary herself had not revealed to anybody, information that only she and the angel were privy to. Elizabeth used the same words the angel used to greet Mary many miles away at the scene of the annunciation. Mary had been favored out of all the women on earth to carry the only Son of the Father. She would not just carry the Son but biologically give Him flesh and blood, which He would later offer as a sacrifice to the Father to atone for the sins of humanity. She was the first woman addressed by a heavenly figure with such praise. Moses had the privilege of talking to God face to face, but Mary had the singular honor not just to touch God in flesh and blood but to bear Him in her womb.

It was now Elizabeth's to express her surprise at the event unfolding before her. Mary must have visited her in the past, and of course, there is nothing strange about someone paying a relative a visit. But to Elizabeth, this particular visit was extraordinary and surprising: "And how does this happen to me that the mother of my Lord should come to me?" (Luke 1:43). She was echoing the voice of the world, as God the Son who "humbled himself taking the form of a slave, coming in human likeness" (Philipians 2:7) to visit us. Her rhetorical question recalls the one David asked when the ark of the Lord was taken to his house; "How can the ark of the Lord come to me?" (2 Samuel 6:9). Mary was showered with heavenly greetings—first from the angel, now from her elderly cousin. Fulton Sheen wrote, "This Salutation came from the mother of the herald to the mother of the King whose path the herald was to prepare."[20] Elizabeth received Mary not as her little cousin but as the chosen one of God.

She then revealed how the babies they were carrying reacted when they heard her greeting. Unknown to Mary, when she greeted Elizabeth, the baby in her womb connected with the baby in Elizabeth's womb, the precursor who would announce Christ's presence to the world. Elizabeth's baby reacted so positively that his elderly mother could feel it. Elizabeth said, "For at the moment the sound of your greeting reached my ears, the infant in my womb leaped for joy" (Luke 1:44). The joy that humanity lost after the fall was now restored—the joy that every person who comes into contact with Christ will share. The sick will be restored to health, the dead will be raised by the Savior, and all will leap for joy, a joy that has no end.

The baby King in the womb of His mother communicated with the baby precursor in the womb of Elizabeth, the baby who would grow up and point out Christ to the world with these words: "Behold, the Lamb of God, who takes away the sin of the world. He is the one of whom I said, 'A man is coming after me who ranks ahead of me because He existed before me" (John 1:29–30). It is interesting to see how one mother and her unborn baby reacted to the presence of another mother and her unborn baby. The babies will meet again as adults, when John will baptize Jesus, and the Father

---

[20] Fulton Sheen, *Life of Christ*, (New York: Image Books, 1999) p. 24.

will confirm His paternity from heaven "This is beloved Son, with whom I am well pleased" (Matthew 3:17).

Elizabeth, in her inspired statement, revealed that a baby in the womb has life and feelings. If he can leap for joy in the face of a pleasant experience, he also can cry in pain when going through an unpleasant experience, such as feeling the doctor's knife during abortion. I wonder what abortion advocates would say.

After the two women exchanged these inspired pleasantries, Mary poured out a poem of praise to God, highlighting His hand in the history of the chosen people:

> My soul proclaims the greatness of the Lord; my spirit rejoices in God my Savior. For He has looked upon His handmaid's lowliness; behold, from now on will all ages call me blessed. The mighty One has done great things for me, and Holy is His name. His mercy is from age to age to those who fear Him. He has shown might with His arm, dispersed the arrogant of mind and heart. He has thrown down the rulers from their thrones but lifted up the lowly. The hungry He has filled with Good things; the rich He has sent away empty. He has helped Israel His servant remembering His Mercy, according to promise to our fathers, to Abraham and His descendants forever. (Luke 1:46–56)

Mary's visit to her cousin Elizabeth presents another interesting scene in the sacred drama of our salvation. Her visit first and foremost brought the good news of the Messiah's arrival to Elizabeth; she thus became the first missionary and evangelist of the gospel of Christ. This scene also portrays Mary not just as our mother but also a role model for us—a model of humility and selfless service. It shows her character as someone who is ready to help others in need, as seen when she intervened at the wedding feast in Cana. Note that the angel only told her about Elizabeth's pregnancy; he did not ask Mary to go on that visit. She did it of her own volition.

One can hardly imagine how a person with her standards, told she would be the mother of God, humbled herself to serve her cousin, who was to give birth to an ordinary human being. One might think that Mary would have wanted Elizabeth to serve her. But to fulfill what the Lord Jesus Himself said later during His teaching—that He came not to be served but to serve—the holy mother showed us the way. She was carrying God in her womb, but she humbled herself to serve the mother of a human being, the forerunner of the God-child she carried, who would later say about Jesus, in a very humble and sincere way: "One mightier than I is coming after me. I am not worthy to stoop and loosen the thongs of his sandals. I have baptized with water; He will baptize you with the Holy Spirit" (Luke 1:7–8).

Just for a moment, as Fulton Sheen puts it, "The handmaid of the Lord becomes the handmaid of Elizabeth."[21] That is

---

[21] Sheen, *The World's First Love*, p. 22.

the way of the Lord, as Jesus himself put it: "The greatest among you must be your servant. Whoever exalts himself will be humbled; but whoever humbles himself will be exalted" (Matthew 23:11–12). This plays out very well in relation to His holy mother.

The Blessed Virgin Mary was richly endowed with the virtue of humility. This virtue makes her stand out among humans and makes it possible, as she put it in the Magnificat, for all of humanity to call her blessed. She understood that, based on what she did and the blessing God gave her, she would be regarded as blessed from generation to generation.

7

All Ages Will Call Me Blessed

Mary is not known as one of the prophets, but she did see the future and spoke about it, inspired by the Spirit of God poured onto her while the Word of God formed in her womb. She knew that, from the moment she agreed to be the mother of the Savior of the world, her status had changed. People no longer would see her as the little virgin from Nazareth; everybody would honor her because of her Son.

Thus, in my opinion, the statement "from now on all ages will call me blessed" began the moment she accepted God's offer. The angel told her that her child would be the Son of the Most High God. The angel himself gave her due honor, to the surprise and amazement of the young Virgin. This is because, as she put it, "The mighty One has done great things for me, and holy is His name." She was blessed because she carried in her womb the Word made flesh, whose coming had been foretold by the prophets long before she was born. With "all ages" she alluded to the fact that all living beings, who are the seeds of the new woman, from generation to generation will accord her the necessary respect. It does not mean a particular denomination should do so, as some modern Christians try to suggest. Her statement also does not mean she was boasting about her prowess or worthiness; rather, she was glorifying God, who chose her due to her humility. Hear her: "For He has looked upon the lowliness of His handmaid," which she believed was the reason she was blessed. She acknowledged her humility before the Almighty, who always has been fond of the lowly. All people of goodwill, regardless of denomination, therefore, should see this as a call to honor the Blessed Virgin Mary. In the early days, people acknowledged her as the greatest woman on earth and honored her as she deserved to be honored.

William Wordsworth was not Catholic, but in 1822 he wrote a poem, "The Virgin," in Mary's honor.

> Mother! Whose virgin bosom was uncrost
> With the least shade of thought to sin allied;
> Woman! Above all women glorified,
> Our tainted nature's solitary boast;
> Purer than foam on central ocean tost;

Brighter than eastern skies at daybreak
strewn
With fancied roses, than the unblemished
moon
Before her wane begins on heaven's blue
coast;
Thy image falls to earth. Yet some, I ween,
Not unforgotten the suppliant knee might
bend,
As to a visible power, in which did blend
All that was mixed and reconciled in Thee
Of mother's love with maiden purity
Of high with low, celestial with Terrence!

The poem glorifies the Blessed Virgin Mary and fulfills her prediction that all ages will call her blessed.

As a young Jew, Jesus understood and obeyed the Ten Commandments, including "honor your father and mother." He honored and obeyed Mary, as the scripture tells us: "He went down with them and came to Nazareth, and was obedient to them …" (Luke 2:51). He honored her as His mother, even though He knew He was God. He knew that honoring His mother did not take away His honor and dignity as God. What we learn from Him is that honoring Mary does not diminish God, who alone deserves our total worship. If Jesus could honor Mary, we too are obliged to honor her. He honored her by respecting her wishes, even turning water to wine at her behest.

Devotion to Mary is a divine directive. Mary, Luke has us believe, was speaking under the influence of the Holy Spirit when she described herself as "blessed." The Holy Spirit was truly at work here; both Elizabeth and the Blessed Virgin Mary were filled with the Holy Spirit. I believe our Blessed Mother knew that, at a point during this salvific drama that had started to unfold, a whole generation of Christians would become her children due to the generosity of her Son. They then would be obliged to honor her as their mother and bless her name as God had blessed her since the beginning of times. Since she was speaking under the influence of the Holy Spirit, it therefore stands that this would be fulfilled. She was a lady who, even when humanity was lost in the darkness of sin, was the only human being on earth honored by God.

The one who was greeted by the angel as favored by God was full of grace even before the Savior who would deliver His people from sin was born. She was holy before the debt of our sins was paid on Calvary. God sent His Son to redeem the world from its sins; Mary was the only living person who was already full of grace before the redemption of humanity. This woman is worthy of our respect. To criticize those who honor Mary not only criticizes God, who first honored her, it insults the Creator of all things, who knows about every individual. Anyone who finds it difficult to honor our Blessed Mother probably has an agenda that was prepared for him by the evil one. At the beginning of time, the devil was told he would be in conflict with the seed of the promised woman. If the woman from whom our Lord Jesus Christ took His human flesh and blood is not worthy of honor and respect, I wonder who is. This same flesh and blood were offered on the cross as a sacrifice to the Father for our redemption; this was the flesh and blood about which Jesus said, "Amen, amen, I say to you, unless you eat the flesh of the Son of Man and drink His blood, you do not have life within you" (John 6:53).

It is worth noting how people who do not have the same biological parentage call themselves brothers and sisters because they belong to the same church. They love and respect one another in this way without raising any eyebrow, but criticize and demonize those who call Mary their mother. I have even heard some people proudly call the wives of their pastors "mother"—"mommy in the Lord"—yet no one criticizes them. My simple explanation for this is that it is the fulfilment of God's statement in the book of Genesis: "I will put enmity between you and the woman, and between your offspring and hers" (Genesis 3:15) Those who call Mary "mother" and accord her due respect also are fulfilling her statement that she would be called "blessed" by all future generations. It is sad when people who don't support the respect accorded to the Blessed Virgin Mary try to compare her with other created human beings. By all indications, Mary is the woman of the book of Genesis, and we who recognize her as mother are the seeds Genesis describes.

Let us take a moment to reflect on her statement: "all ages will call me blessed." Why doesn't that statement ring true today? As far as I know, only a few Christians recognize her as blessed. What is wrong? It is obvious that those who find it difficult to honor her—and even go against those who give her the honor she is due—are among those who the Lord God himself described to the devil: "I will put enmity between you and the woman, between her seed and yours." Those who fight against Mary are the seeds of the other. That is why they can't call her blessed, they can't call her holy, they can't call her mother. They don't want to be identified with her. This statement of the Blessed Virgin was prompted by the Holy Spirit, and those opposed to it are definitely on the opposite side of the divide. The Virgin who was honored by a heavenly figure—God's messenger—is denied that same due honor by mere mortals, because they still belong to the old Eve who was arrogant enough to challenge the authority of God.

Mary, the New Ark of the Covenant

In the old dispensation, the Ark of the Covenant that carried the tablets of stones on which the hand of God inscribed the Ten Commandments was deemed to be holy. In much the same way, the womb carrying the word of God made flesh is holy too. In the case of the Ark of the Covenant, God told Moses which materials to use to construct the ark: "You shall make an ark of acacia wood, two and a half cubits long, one and a half cubits wide, and a half cubit high" (Exodus 25:10). This was done to make it holy and special. "The Ark of the Covenant was made of an indestructible wood," writes Reverend Cornelius J. O'Connell, "while Mary never suffered at any moment of her life the destructible influence of even the original sin."[22]

God also took time to prepare the person who would carry His own Word made flesh. Her womb would serve as a tabernacle, where Jesus would hibernate for nine months. As with the Ark of the Covenant, the Word made flesh who

---

[22] C. J. O'Connell, *Holy Mary: Getting To Know and Love Our Blessed Mother Through Her Magnificent Titles* (Baltimore, MD: John Murphy Company, 2016), p. 83.

would be the bread of life would be kept there throughout the period of gestation. Bishop Barron puts it so well here: "Just as the Holy of Holies in the temple was kept pure and inviolate. So the definitive temple, the true Ark of the Covenant, which is Mary herself, should all the more be untrammeled."[23]

The Ark of the Covenant was considered sacred. Similarly, the Blessed Virgin Mary is considered holy and should be called "blessed," as she prophesied in the Magnificat: "Behold all generations shall call me blessed." Treating the Blessed Virgin Mary like any other woman is the same as respecting only the content in the Ark of the Covenant and treating the ark itself like any other wooden box. Scott Hahn makes a beautiful comparison between Mary and the Ark of the Covenant: "Whatever made the ark holy made Mary even Holier. If the first ark contained the word of God in stone, Mary's body contained the word of God enfleshed."[24]

In the Magnificat, the Blessed Virgin Mary mouthed the script written by the Holy Spirit as soon as the Lord created her in a special way with a very special mission. God has the ability of turning even something mundane into a sacred object for the glory of His name. When the Jewish people bragged about having Abraham as their father, John the Baptist scolded them and told them God could do the unthinkable: "And do not presume to say to yourselves, 'we have Abraham as a father.' For I tell you, God can raise up children to Abraham from these stones" (Matthew 3:9). If

---

[23] Barron, *Catholicism*, p. 100.

[24] Hahn, *Hail, Holy Queen*, pp. 60–61.

God could make children out of stones, would He not be able to create a special person who would give pure and untainted flesh to His Word when the time came for Him to come into the world?

Mary's elderly cousin, during their visit, may have watched her as she spoke and wondered where she obtained such wisdom and the ability to highlight God's work to the people of Israel in a carefully crafted poetic verses. She was a young lady, yet the wisdom packed into those words was beyond her age. This was because she carried the wisdom of God in her womb. She had just spoken with an angel who told her about the role the Holy Spirit would play in the fulfilment of the promise. The Holy Spirit had started to work within her, so one can safely say that she was speaking under the Spirit's influence. She recounted the people's history and linked it to their future: "from now on, all ages will call me blessed."

Mary recognized the great works produced by God in the history of man. His greatness could not be measured. She particularly extoled the spiritual benefits God had endowed upon her. In the inspired poem, she does not say "I proclaim" but "my soul proclaims," a reference to her inner being. The proclamation resulted from her deep union with God in her heart and mind, which marks a contrast to those who only present an outward show for others to see, about whom the Lord Jesus would say, "This people honors me with their lips, but their hearts are far from me" (Matthew 15:8). God had used a similar statement to repudiate some people through the mouth of prophet Isaiah: "Since this people draws near with words only and honor me with their lips alone, though their hearts are far from me ..." (Isaiah 29:13).

The Blessed Virgin Mary, whose soul had been purified since she was born, offered this adoration to the One who created her. Calling to mind the greeting of the angel, she rejoiced in God her savior. This could only come from someone who truly acknowledged the power and work of God in her life. So, in the opening sentence of her poem of praise, the Magnificat, she glorifies and praises the great works of the almighty God in her life.

For three months, as these noble women stayed together under one roof, the mother of a King was serving the mother of His subject; this truly showed the reality of God's immense love. He serves in humility. Both women had one thing in common; they were both carrying their first children, though one was older and the other younger. What would have happened to Elizabeth if Mary was not there to handle her chores? We do not know, but God instilled in the heart of this young lady the character to help someone in need. She started preaching the gospel of her Son, helping the needy even before the King was born. During Mary's three-month stay in the house of Zachariah, there must have been a lot of communication between the two children in their wombs, which enabled the baby King to lay out His salvific mission to the baby precursor.

Mary stayed with Elizabeth for three months, the exact number of months that the Ark of the Covenant remained in the house of Obededom. This confirms that Mary was the new Ark of the Covenant.

8

She Brought Forth the Savior

It is interesting to note that Mary did not give birth to her child in the city of Nazareth where she and Joseph resided. They may have made some preparations for the child to be born there, but the will of God offered something different. They had to undertake a journey, compelled by a decree issued by Augustus Caesar for a mandatory census. In obedience, Joseph and Mary went to the City of David to be counted. It was a journey they did not volunteer to take on their own, As Pope Francis puts it, "The road that Mary and Joseph take to Bethlehem, in obedience to the imperial order, is a road of humility. Mary is humble; she 'does not understand' but 'leaves her soul to the will of God.'"[25] This happened so that the will of God as prophesied by the prophet—that the King would be born in Bethlehem—might be fulfilled. Mary's journey was one of obedience, prompted by humility through faith in God, beginning at the annunciation when she accepted the Will of God without knowing what lay ahead. Whatever she did was

---

[25] Francis, *Encountering the Truth: Meeting God in the Everyday* (New York: Image Books, 2015), p.11.

because of her faith in God, and everything came to pass as arranged by God. That fateful night while they were in the city of Bethlehem, it came to pass: the Savior of the world was born.

What a night! It was a night that God predestined to change human history forever, and yet there was nothing extraordinary about it. It was as quiet as any other night, with the stars shining brightly. The inhabitants of the world had all gone to bed, except for the holy family, who had a sacred mission and were expecting the Savior of the world, and the shepherds, who were blessed to be the first humans to hear the good news of the birth of the Savior. It was in the middle of the night, and darkness had descended over the whole world, putting every living soul into a deep slumber, the kind of sleep that enveloped Adam when God made a helpmate for him. When the new light came into the world, taking on our flesh, He brought a light into the previously darkened world, which was literally in darkness when He arrived. Mary, the chosen mother of this divine light, brought forth a Savior. The people's long wait had finally come to an end. She gave birth to the Son of God, the Savior of the human race.

Today, we do not adore Mary, because she gave birth to a child. Childbearing is a biological function of womanhood, but we adore her because she gave birth to a unique personality, the Son of God. Naturally she was a woman like any other, a mother like any other, but by God's arrangement, she was "full of grace," and of all women she was the most favored. The birth of her Son brought about a new birth to the history of humanity. And so all generations now call her "blessed."

When people try to equate Mary with any ordinary woman, they are missing the point. That is what has led to so much misunderstanding about Mary in the non-Catholic communities. Mary, however, has been misunderstood. Unless one has a divine enlightenment, one is likely to hold a misconception about her. Even her husband, Joseph, probably saw her as an ordinary woman, subject to the natural procreation order, and was concerned when he found her to be with child, although they had never been together, which is the natural way. He reacted as any husband would have until he experienced a divine intervention that calmed his nerves.

Here is the likely scenario that must have led to Joseph's reaction. Saint Luke tells us that Mary went to visit Elizabeth, who was with child. She may not have had time to tell Joseph about her encounter with the angel Gabriel. She spent three months with Elizabeth before she returned home. Joseph must have been shocked to see his betrothed three month's pregnant. He thought she had cheated on him, and since, as the scripture says, "he was a righteous man, yet unwilling to expose her to shame, decided to divorce her quietly"(Matthew 1:19). It was at this point that an angel let him know that his betrothed was not just an ordinary woman; she had been chosen by God to bear the Son of God, and everything was according to God's plan:

> Such was his intention when, behold, the angel of the Lord appeared to him in a dream and said, "Joseph, son of David, do not be afraid to take Mary, your wife, into your home. For it is through the holy Spirit that this child has been conceived in her.

> She will bear a son, and you are to name
> Him Jesus, because He will save His people
> from their sins." (Matthew 1:20–21)

Until the angel appeared, Joseph was thinking from his human point of view. He saw Mary as an ordinary woman. The angel was the divine intervention he needed. This was how Joseph learned about the coming of Jesus through his betrothed. At this point, he understood the mission of the woman to whom he was married. He was ready to cooperate with her so the Will of God would be fulfilled in the world. Mary was not an ordinary woman; she was favored by God and full of grace. Unless Christians understand this, the controversy over the honor given to Mary by Catholics will continue.

The mystery of the incarnation ushered in our salvation; it was a turning point in the history of humanity. All Christians celebrate and hail the incarnation, but sometimes we leave out a very important person—the one who bore the Son of God, the Blessed Virgin Mary. Most Protestants don't believe that she played any significant role in the mystery of the incarnation, which loses sight of a prominent aspect of salvation history. That is probably why Pope Saint John Paul said, "And one cannot think of the reality of the incarnation without referring to Mary, the mother of the incarnate word." [26]

Her yes was a very important response in the salvation history. She carried the Word made flesh in her womb. It was now time for the Son of God "to touch down"

---

[26] John Paul II, *Redemptoris Mater*, n.5.

the countdown started when the holy couple set out for Bethlehem:

> In those days a decree went out from Caesar Augustus that the whole world should be enrolled. This was the first enrollment, when Quirinius was governor of Syria. So all went to be enrolled, each to his own town. And so Joseph too went up from Galilee from the town of Nazareth to Judea, to the city of David that is called Bethlehem, because he was of the house and family of David to be enrolled with Mary his betrothed, who was with child. While they were there, the time came for her to have a child, and she gave birth to her firstborn Son. She wrapped Him in swaddling clothes and laid Him in a manger, because there was no room for them in the inn. (Luke 2:1–7)

The prophecy of Isaiah now was fulfilled. God, Immanuel, is here with us. The young mother did what Moses and the other ancient patriarchs could not do. God told Moses, "But my face you cannot see, for no man sees me and lives" (Exodus 33:20). Mary saw the face of God and continued to live. She touched God, she nursed God—a rare privilege reserved for one who was highly favored by God. Her caring role began as soon as she "wrapped the child in swaddling clothes." The Creator now was being taken care of by the created. He lay there, sleeping among animals, awaiting His first human visitors, the shepherds.

Simultaneously, another event was going on in heaven. The angels were singing and praising God, who had once again showed favor to humans through the birth of His Son. A detachment of angels was dispatched to the earth to deliver the breaking news to the shepherds who were in the field tending their flock. This was a sign that the new King would have to shepherd another kind of flock. The kings and princes of the world were enjoying their sleep in comfortable suites in the same city when the King of Kings arrived the world. He arrived not with pomp and pageantry but privately in a manger. The holy couple and the animals in the manger were His first companions in the world. Mary took care of Him because He was her child and at the same time adored Him as her God. She was the channel through which the Savior of the world came to His subjects. She knew what this meant and was prepared right from the moment she uttered her brief acceptance speech, "Behold, I am the handmaid of the Lord. May it be done to me according to your Word" (Luke 1:38). She knew about the inconveniences she would have to experience due to this mission, which had just started. Delivering a human baby in a manger was not normal, but she knew that was what fate had brought her way.

There is nothing as exciting as unexpected good news. Sometimes the recipient's reaction is hilarious. A person might shout, "No, it's a lie!" or "Are you serious?" when the news seems too good to be true. The people had waited for centuries for God to fulfill His promise to their forebears. When they heard that the promise has been fulfilled, the shepherds were excited.

The shepherds had turned up for their routine duty—to watch over the flock at night. They did not expect anything unusual to happen; they must have spent their time talking, laughing, and engaging in some activities to keep themselves awake. All of a sudden a supernatural phenomenon unfolded before them: a heavenly figure appeared, which understandably sent them into a panic. It was an angel from heaven. The angel calmed their nerves before he broke the news to them: "Do not be afraid, for behold, I proclaim to you good news of great joy that will be for all the people" (Luke 2:10).

Their fear turned into expectant anxiety, and they were all ears to receive this "news of great joy." At this point, I do not know if any of them even had time to think about Isaiah's prophecy, which had stated that a virgin would conceive and bear a child. Who knows what truly was on their minds. They must have thought about many things, except the one occurring at that moment: God had taken flesh and would dwell among them. They must have wondered what kind of news would give "great joy for all the people." The angel did not wait for their imaginations to go wild before he broke the news to them: "For today in the City of David, a Savior has been born for you, who is Messiah and Lord" (Luke 2:11).

The angel knew Mary had performed her first motherly actions to protect the child from cold by wrapping Him in swaddling clothes. He gave the shepherds a sign that they could use to identify the newborn Messiah: "And this will be a sign for you; you will find an infant wrapped in swaddling clothes and lying in a manger" (Luke 2:12).

When the angel finished delivering the message, he departed from them. The shepherds may have looked at each other, as if to say, "Is this for real? The Savior we have been waiting for has been born among us? What are we waiting for? Let's go right away." They left the flock in the fields and went to the City of David to behold the true Shepherd who had been born as a baby, as the angel had told them. Once the Will of God comes into one's heart, it alters one's personal agenda. They went in haste and arrived at the location of the nativity—not a suite for important personalities or a well-furnished maternity ward where children of the rich are born, but a manger where animals are kept. That would have been enough to discourage anybody, but the shepherds were encouraged when they saw the things the angel had described. They found "Mary and Joseph and the infant lying in the manger" (Luke 2:16).

They were so excited, they started describing what had taken place during the night as they kept watch over their flock—how they had been visited by an angel, their first encounter with a supernatural being, who delivered the breaking news to them. With all the excitement they could muster, they explained what the angels had told them about the child. They probably expected their listeners to be equally excited. They must have been disappointed when they did not see similar excitement come from Mary, the mother of the child. In their minds, they must have thought that what they said did not make any sense to the holy family. They did not know that both parents, especially Mary, had prior knowledge of all the shepherds were saying. Mary kept this knowledge in her heart.

The shepherds, I guess, were privileged to be the first set of human beings, beyond the holy family, to see the Savior of the world. To an ordinary eye, He would have seemed to be an ordinary Jewish baby, born in an extraordinary place. He would have to grow up that way, hidden to the normal eye, and only revealed to a privileged few. He would grow up to tell Peter later: "For flesh and blood has not revealed this to you but my heavenly Father" (Matthew 16:17). Mary was given the task to care for Him until the appointed hour. Her heart became the storage facility for messianic secrets. Later, during His public ministry, Jesus cautioned His disciples "not to tell anybody" anything that was within the messianic secrecy.

Mary's ability to store these things in her heart was due to her humility, for it takes a truly humble person to keep secrets, especially when telling them will boost one's ego. Despite all that had happened to her, was revealed to her, and was unfolding before her, she did not see the need to divulge information to others, because she saw herself as a lowly handmaid, an undeserving recipient of favors from God. She had been given her role—to be a mother to the Son of God who came to save humanity. The shepherds saw a woman who had just given birth to the baby Savior, but in reality she was more than that: she was a custodian of the living God in the flesh. The shepherds thought they were giving information to a human whose knowledge was limited, not knowing that because Mary had been chosen to bear the Son of God, she had received information about the salvation plan firsthand from God. She had the security clearance that allowed her to see the classified documents related to the plan. She was given the ability to hold these things and "ponder … them in her heart."

Any ordinary family would have been proud to showcase their child if he had been blessed to be outstanding in class and perform well in his field. They would not hide him from the public, but since God's ways are not like human ways, Mary hid Jesus from prying eyes and ears in the world around them. Thus, the world was kept in the dark until the appointed "hour.

Mary does not speak much in the Gospels, but her actions tell us much about her role in the salvation history of mankind. In most cases, we meet her on a journey—to the hill country to meet Elizabeth, with Joseph to the City of David for a census and to have her child, to the temple for the dedication of the infant Jesus, with the whole family as they fled to Egypt, on her pilgrimage to Jerusalem where the young Jesus got lost in the temple. These journeys all culminated in the one she took with her Son on the way to Calvary. Mary's life was full of journeys rather than speeches.

Because all that she did was in the service of the Word, she preached more by her actions than her words; that's why she did not speak much in the Gospels. She only spoke to designated individuals and on select occasions. The first time she spoke was during her interaction with the angel Gabriel; then she recited her poem of praise to God, the Magnificat, before Elizabeth. When the shepherds recounted their encounter with the angels and how everything had happened just like the angels told them, everybody was amazed but Mary did not speak. She knew there was more to it than what they saw with their physical eyes.

Mary, like many other first-time mothers, must have had to learn the rudiments of nursing a baby and her other maternal responsibilities. However, the spiritual responsibilities that were imposed on her in the plan of salvation had been handled from the beginning: "the Holy Spirit will come upon you." The Spirit did not leave her but guided her all the way to her final moment with her Son on Calvary, when He handed her over to us: "Son," He said to John, "behold your mother."(John 19:26). She must have realized, however, that her role in the plan of salvation did not end with the death of Jesus on the cross but would continue with God's adopted children, who through the ministry of the apostles would come to believe in God through His Son. These were the people He prayed for during His priestly prayer: "I pray not only for them, but also for those who will believe in me through their word" (John 17:20).

Mary and Joseph likely taught Jesus the ways of a human family, like house chores, and Joseph may have shown Him how to do carpentry. The boy who grew up in a carpenter's family ended up nailed to a wooden object made by a carpenter. Mary must have watched with admiration when little Jesus played with the wood in the carpenter's shop. Then she watched in agony as the adult Jesus bled to death on a wooden cross in an open arena, bringing to completion the prophecy of the sword given by Simeon when she and Joseph presented the baby Jesus in the temple. Her journey through the salvation history of humanity did not stop with Christ's death and burial; she continues to suffer for her children in the church, who break her heart when they disobey Jesus and give glory to the evil one. She told this to the three little shepherd children in Fatima and encouraged them to make reparations to appease Jesus's heart.

9

She Carried the Lord into the Temple

The Blessed Virgin Mary is the most important of all created beings, and she is first in everything in all aspects of her life. She is the first and only human being to physically carry God in her arms into the temple of worship. God was spiritually present in the temple, but Mary brought God in flesh and blood there to interact with humans who worshiped Him. This action alone was enough to make all the ages call her blessed. Jesus even blessed the eyes of those who had the opportunity to see Him: "But blessed are your eyes, because they see … Amen, I say to you, many prophets and righteous people longed to see what you see but did not see it …" (Matthew 13:16-17). How then could the one who carried Him to the temple not be blessed?

On many occasions in her life, the Blessed Virgin Mary entered the temple, either to pray with her parents or to pray on her own. Her parents even allowed her to work in the temple, but this particular visit was unique in several ways. On the other occasions, she went to the temple to worship God, but this time she had God in her arms. The God she had worshiped in the Spirit went with her in the flesh into the temple. The Lord of the Sabbath was taken into the temple by someone who, by the special grace of God, shared His flesh and blood and protected Him as a mother. That is why, of all women, she is the most blessed, the singular privilege that belongs to the mother of the Creator. It takes the grace of God to understand the position of the Blessed Mother in the history of human salvation.

When she carried Jesus into the temple, our Blessed Virgin Mary first and foremost did it as a mother's duty. The Blessed Virgin Mary, though still very young compared to the old dispensation figures, made history as the first human being to physically carry the Lord into the temple of the Lord. She was blessed in all ramifications. Before the Blessed Mother took Jesus into the temple, the people worshiped the Lord in Spirit there. The Blessed Virgin Mary carried Him into the temple to fulfill Mosaic law:

> When the days were completed for their purification, according to the law of Moses, they took Him to Jerusalem to present Him to the Lord, just as it is written in the law of the Lord, "Every male that opens the womb shall be consecrated to the Lord" and to offer the sacrifice of "a pair of turtledoves or two young pigeons" in accordance with the dictate in the law of the Lord. (Luke 2:22–24)

She may have done this as a divine duty, but in essence, Jesus entered the temple to fulfill the prophecy. Mary, therefore, performed both her maternal responsibility and a prophetic one. As a child born into a Jewish family, Jesus fulfilled the human responsibility to be purified in the temple, even though He did not need to. In the same way, he did not need to be baptized by John but did so to fulfill His human responsibility. As God, He entered the temple on His own to fulfill the prophecy. In the temple, many people saw Him as a little child taken by the parents to perform the Mosaic rite of purification. Others, however, saw the God for whom they had been waiting for entering the temple in fulfillment of a prophecy. Simeon and the prophetess Anna were endowed with the Holy Spirit to confirm this fulfillment, and they spoke out as the Spirit directed them.

In her role as a mother, Mary combined both the spiritual and the biological responsibilities of the baby Jesus. She cuddled Him for eight days and prepared to present Him in the temple. Despite the fact that she knew He that had been born to her, was called Son of the living God, and was Holy, she did not count herself and her family exempt from the religious law or the custom of the people. She knew that, according the law, any firstborn child had to be dedicated to the Lord. Jesus was her first child, and so He had to be offered to the Lord; this was the same child who later on in His adult life would describe Himself as "the Lord of the Sabbath." She nursed Him for eight days, and then it was time to set out from their hometown of Galilee to Jerusalem for the required ritual of dedication. In her human thinking, Mary must have wondered what would happen when they presented the Lord in the temple. That, however, did not deter her, as she had surrendered her will to the Lord when she agreed to bring forth the Son of God. As they entered the temple, God's preplanned agenda for this scene kicked off. Simeon, a devout man who had been promised that he would behold the salvation of Israel, was directed by the Holy Spirit to be in the temple at that moment. Perhaps the words of the prophet Malachi were whispered into his ears: "And suddenly there will come to the temple the Lord whom you seek" (Malachi 3:1).

God lined up a number of individuals to star in this great drama of our salvation; some played lead roles, and many others played supporting roles. Simeon was given the role of reinterpreting the child not just to His mother but to all those waiting for the salvation of Israel. He was the second person in the lineup of those who would announce the presence of God in the flesh. Earlier, Elizabeth announced His arrival through His mother and that the child in her womb had reacted to the presence of the "mother of my Lord." Simeon welcomed Him into the temple and took the child from His mother; for the first time since this child had been born eight days earlier, the child Jesus left His mother's hands and was put in some other person's hands. He held the child and prayed to the God who always keeps His promise to His people. Simeon is not numbered among the prophets, but his statement in the temple was nothing short of a prophesy. He started with prayers:

> Now, Master, you may let your servant go
> in peace, according to your word, for my
> eyes have seen your salvation, which you
> prepared in sight of all the peoples, a light
> for the revelation to the Gentiles, and glory
> for your people Israel. (Luke 2:29–32)

After praising God, Simeon made a stunning statement about the child and then told Mary what neither the angel

Gabriel nor Elizabeth had told her about her role in the salvation plan. Simeon gave his own prophesy to the Blessed Mother:

> Behold, this child is destined for the fall and rise of many in Israel, and to be a sign that will be contradicted. And you yourself a sword will pierce, so that the thoughts of many hearts may be revealed. (Luke 2:34–35)

Simeon's message to Mary left her pondering those words in her heart. Sometimes the word of God could be too heavy to bear. Simeon in his temple testimony revealed certain things that the angel had not mentioned at the annunciation, which made Mary ponder. Pope Saint John Paul was right when he said, "Simeon's words seem like a second annunciation to Mary." While the angel announced that she would be the mother of God, Simeon announced what she would go through as the mother of God.

Another character in this salvation drama stepped forward to say her lines regarding the mission of the new baby—the prophetess Anna—who "gave thanks to God and spoke about the child to all who were waiting the redemption of Jerusalem" (Luke 2:38).

All these statements about this baby would have been enough to make a young mother panic; after all, she had not bargained for this. The statements were mostly pregnant with meaning, beginning with the words of the annunciation, the praise of Elizabeth, the description of the shepherds, and the words from Simeon. But knowing she had already told God she was His handmaid and had asked to be used according to the will of the Lord, she had no option. She had to ponder all these statements in her hearts. Mary had already started carrying—in the form of these heavy words—the heavy wooden cross that her Son would carry on His shoulders on the way to Calvary. She carried this heavy load on her journey with Christ throughout His earthly life. Standing beside the cross of her bleeding child as He was dying was the heaviest of the crosses she had to carry with her Son on His journey.

The presentation had more to do with Mary's obedience to the law. Jesus, at that moment, could not have carried Himself into the temple. Mary and Joseph had to take the credit. Again, if she had not gone to the temple, she would not have learned what would befall her on her journey along with her Son. Simeon was given these messages for her about the child Jesus, and the only place to deliver them was in the temple. Her suffering alongside her Son was in her package when she agreed to bear the Son of God. After the revelation, she could only treasure all that in her heart.

Of all the people present in the temple that day, it was the Blessed Virgin Mary who received an unpleasant message: "a sword will pierce your heart." A woman who had gone through such hard times to nurse the child who would redeem humanity deserves at least some measure of respect and honor from humans, the beneficiaries of this great work of salvation.

10

The Night Flight to Egypt

When they had departed, behold, the angel of the Lord appeared to Joseph in a dream and said, "Rise, and take the child and His mother, flee to Egypt, and stay there until I tell you. Herod is going to search for the

> child to destroy Him." Joseph rose and
> took the child and His mother by night
> and departed for Egypt. (Matthew 2:13–14)

Egypt has a very interesting history when it comes to God's relationship with His people, beginning with the ancient people of God. The first-generation people of God, the children of Israel, went into Egypt to escape the famine that threatened to wipe them off the face of the earth. As it turned out, they were enslaved by the Egyptians. It is interesting to note here that God had to use a strong hand to deliver His people from Egypt into freedom. If God used a strong hand to get His people out of Egypt, how could He ask Joseph to take his child into Egypt for refuge? Maybe God wanted to show that there was a new beginning in Jesus Christ.

The holy family—the progenitors of the new people of God, the new Israel, courtesy of the redemptive work of Christ—went to Egypt to escape Herod's threat of the murder, which hovered over the new baby. This, Matthew said, fulfilled the prophecy of Hosea: "When Israel was a child I loved him, out of Egypt I called my son" (Hosea 11:1). This prophecy, which originally referred to the people of Israel, Matthew saw in their flight, a new exodus with a new Moses. The flight to Egypt was another cross the holy family had to bear, one they did not anticipate but was within the package the Blessed Mother received at the annunciation. Mary combined the protective instinct of a mother and a dedication to her vocation to respond to the Will of God as she embarked on this nocturnal journey.

Before our Blessed Lord carried His cross, the Blessed Virgin Mary was carrying her own cross alongside Jesus. One of the crosses she carried was to wake up in the middle of the night, at the instruction of an angel, and flee to Egypt with Joseph to ensure the safety of the baby Jesus. The joy of the nativity now changed to the pain of anxiety. When one considers that Mary, who had given birth only a few days earlier, was subjected to such a long night journey to save the baby, it is clear that her strength to do could come only from God, to whom she had dedicated herself to as the "handmaid of the Lord." A queen would not have woken up in the middle of the night to undertake a long journey to save a future king, but that was exactly what Mary did. This shows the difference. His "kingdom is not of this world," and Mary was not the mother of the worldly king.

Let's look at the scenario here. Night is a time to rest, not to make a long-distance journey, certainly not with a little baby who is a few weeks old. Mary and the baby Jesus had gone to bed, hoping to have a wonderful night of rest, but this was not to be. The young King deserved a comfortable rest on the cushion in His little crib but could not enjoy it. Danger was knocking, and the holy family had to move out in the dead of the night because an earthly king was seeking to destroy a heavenly King. An angel of the Lord warned Joseph about the secret plan of the king to kill the child. Right from His infancy, His mother went through hard times to keep Him safe. It was not in her plan to get up in the night and embark on a cross-country walk to another nation to escape the ill design of an evil king. But it became imperative for the safety of the baby. The people He came to save were in their beds, sleeping peacefully, and had no idea that their Savior was heading toward a neighboring nation, so that He could live to fulfill His mission. One can hardly imagine what went through the minds of the parents as they walked along in the quiet of the night. One thing is very clear here, it was not a jolly ride. There were no buses, trains, or cars. They had to walk. They were afraid because the life of the Savior was endangered, and in the dark of night they fled into safety.

This event at the beginning of the King's life was directly opposite to the event at the end of His life, when the hour came. Then He would voluntarily walk at night to Mount Olivet to fulfill the Will of the Father. "Then, after singing a hymn, they went out to the Mount of Olives. Then Jesus said to them, 'This night all of you will have your faith in me shaken, for it is written: I will strike the shepherd, and the sheep of the flock will be dispersed'" (Matthew 26:31). Mary walked through the earlier night that the later night might be fulfilled. If she and Joseph had not acted that night, the last night would not have come. If the baby Jesus had not survived that night, the night in the Mount of Olives would not have occurred. God protected them on that first night so that all would be protected after the later night. Two important nights: one night He took a journey for safety, and on the other He voluntarily walked on a journey to His death. Let me take some time here to look at the nights in Jesus's life. He was born in the night,. It was at night when the angel instructed his father to take the child and the mother to Egypt. Jesus was arrested at night. Finally, He was resurrected at night; the women who came in the morning only saw an empty tomb.

A cross-country walk is not an easy task in the day; consider how much harder it is at night, when you are trying to escape an imminent danger. To appreciate this sacrifice of the holy family, one has to imagine the baby Jesus in His mother's arm, probably asleep, as they walked in the dead of night with Joseph, on the way to a strange land to escape the evil intentions of Herod. This was not a typical trip or a picnic, but a flight to safety for the infant child. Mary must have been pondering the words of Simeon—that a sword would pierce her heart, and the child had been made for the rise and fall of many in Israel. She certainly knew that she was carrying the promised Messiah in her arms as they walked to Egypt, but what lay ahead was still dark in her mind, as the dark night that surrounded them. All her strength was in the statement she uttered at the annunciation: "Behold, I am the handmaid of the Lord, let it be done to me according to thy Word."

11

The Boy Jesus in the Temple

Mary and Joseph did everything to bring up the baby Jesus in the tradition of their forefathers, that is, according to the law of Moses. Although they knew Jesus was God, they did not take things for granted. Every Jewish person was expected to visit Jerusalem at least once a year for the Passover Feast. When Jesus was twelve, His parents fulfilled their religious duty by taking Him to the temple, not knowing they were actually taking Him to perform His Father's business. As good parents and good and devoted Jews, they were set on doing what was necessary. Only God and the twelve-year-old Jesus knew that this trip would be another teachable moment for Mary and Joseph.

Jesus obviously knew what the outcome of the journey to the temple would be, and He intended to make it happen, because He stayed in Jerusalem after the religious function. Mary and Joseph finished everything, as tradition demanded, and were on their way back home when they discovered that Jesus was not with them. A mother's instinct set in, and Mary got worried; then she and Joseph returned to Jerusalem to search for their boy. It must have been a journey overshadowed with fear about what might have happened to her Son. Mary must have been overwhelmed by the anxiety of a mother searching for her child but also of a soul searching for God.

At this point, she prefigured those who later felt emptiness in their souls and went in search of Christ the Savior. Christ's personality has the power to attract empty souls. When people feel the absence of God in their souls, they run in search of Him. In the words of the psalmist, "As the deer longs for streams of water, so my soul longs for you my God" (Psalm 42:2). Some people in the Gospels express this through their activities. Mary Magdalene felt that emptiness when she got up early in the morning to go the tomb of Jesus (Mark 16:1). The woman known as a public sinner felt that emptiness when she entered the house where Jesus was a guest and cried at his feet, wiping them with her hair so that the Lord could clean her soul and fill it with His love (Luke 7:36). It was such emptiness that made Nicodemus sneak out in the night to meet Jesus (John 3:1–15). Curiosity made the disciples of John the Baptist follow Jesus and ask, "Rabbi where do you stay?" Jesus answered, "Come, and you will see" (John 1:35–39). The rich tax collector Zacchaeus, despite his riches, knew he lacked something—the inner peace that only Christ could give— so he climbed a tree just to see Him and was rewarded when the Lord paid a visit to his home (Luke 19:1–10). A Christian who has lost divine grace through sin will feel such emptiness and run to Christ for cleansing and refill.

Mary, filled with anxiety and hurrying to look for Jesus in the temple, teaches us how to look for Jesus whenever we lose sight of Him. One can only imagine how worried she was as she frantically searched the length and breadth of the temple area, anxiety written all over her face. At that time, nothing mattered to her more than her precious little Son, on whom rested the salvation of the human race. His disappearance would spell doom and halt God's plan for humanity. Thus, her anxiety was not just for her Son but for the fulfillment of the plan of God. Mary's quick decision to search for Jesus gives us a lesson in spirituality. It teaches us to take prompt action once we notice we've lost connection with our Savior, who is the way, the truth, and the life.

They searched for three days, a torturous three days, which prefigured the days that Mary would grieve as her child lay in the tomb. They finally found Him in the temple with a group of people they had least expected—a gathering of doctors. He was sitting among the doctors, a sitting position that suggested He was a teacher. They had always known that He was a special child but did not expect Him to manifest His traits so soon. With the doctors, He did not just sit there like a lost child, crying and shaking in fear, waiting for His parents to pick Him up. He was not terrified or nervous among such elites, as any child of His age would be. To Mary and Joseph's surprise, He was actively engaging the doctors, questioning them and taking questions from them, like a celebrated Jewish scholar. He controlled the discussion, while the long-bearded teachers of the law gaped at Him in utter amazement at His wisdom, for they had never witnessed a thing like that in their lives. It would be an understatement to say that the poor and unknown parents of Jesus who saw that scene play out before them were shocked. A big lesson, for both the family and the doctors of law in the temple, came when His mother asked why He had made them worry and search for Him. "Son, why have you done this to us? Your father and I have been looking for you with great anxiety" (Luke 2:48).

Mary asked the question in a very respectful manner. She already respected His mission. One would have expected the child to be sorry for giving His parents a hard time. Instead He gave a shocking response, one marked by authority that no one in the group dared protest; instead, they were speechless before this young King. "Why were you looking for me? Did you not know that I must be in my Father's house?" (Luke 2:49).

"Did you not know …" meant "you should have known better; this thing has been revealed to you." As Jesus would tell His apostles later in life, "Because knowledge of the mysteries of the kingdom of heaven has been granted to you" (Matthew 13:11). He wanted to take Mary down the memory lane—from the annunciation, to her visit to Elizabeth, to Simeon's statement in the temple. Given these earlier events, she should not have been surprised to see Him with the doctors.

The response notwithstanding, Luke says that He went home with His parents and was obedient to them. When He told them that He had to do His Father's business, He was giving them, especially His mother, a hint that more such moments would come. Just when Mary probably thought she knew all about this wonder boy, He kept surprising them with one lesson or another. Each time Mary went into the temple with her child, she always came out with new knowledge about her boy and the mission she had accepted. The first time was at the presentation when Simeon had told her what the angel had not, i.e., what would befall her as a mother of the Son of God. Now she was learning more from the boy Himself, that His mission to do the work of His Father was more important than biological family ties.

He started asserting His independence at the age of twelve to be able to execute the mission of His heavenly Father. The typical mother would be very disturbed to hear her twelve-year-old say she should not bother about Him after He had disappeared for almost three days. But Simeon had warned Mary she would go through a lot, so I guess it was clear to her that she would have to live with this all the days of this child's life. As a young mother, this would have been very traumatic, but as a lady "full of grace," she was able to shoulder whatever came her way. She faithfully accepted her position as the mother of God.

This seems to have been when Jesus began to take control of His mission. Later in His ministry He identified with the flock when someone said:

> "Your mother and your brothers are standing outside, asking to speak with you." But He said in reply to one who told Him, "Who is my mother? Who are my brothers?" And stretching out His hand toward His disciple, He said, "Here are my mother and my brothers. For whoever does the will of my heavenly Father is my brother, and my sister, and mother." (Matthew 12:47–50).

The Blessed Mother was well equipped to handle all these strong statements about or from her Son in the temple area.

Her role in this salvific journey of her Son was very clear. She never complained about all these events; she "treasured all these in her heart." No wonder all ages would continue to call her blessed. All those who are truly gifted with the knowledge about our salvation history will never fail to call her so, because He that is mighty did great things for her.

as it looks, has caused a lot of controversy in the Christian fold. Not all the Christians believe in this teaching. They believe Mary gave birth to Jesus but do not believe that she is the mother of God.

I had an argument with a Protestant friend who denies that Mary is the mother of God; he argued that if Mary were the mother of God, the angel would have said so at the annunciation. But Gabriel only said she would conceive and bear a Son and call Him Jesus. This is a very common dispute between Protestants and Catholics, for whom Mary is a point of dispute.

Some non–Catholics believe that it is a sacrilege to say that Mary, a mere mortal, is the mother of God. I think it's a blasphemy to say that she is not, because that means that Jesus is not God. As the passage from the gospel of John confirms, there is no doubt that Christ is God, and that makes Mary the mother of God. Isaiah's prophesy was " … and He shall be called Immanuel, meaning 'God is with us.'" The prophet could have said "the Son of God is with us." It goes in line with what John said, i.e., that the Word became "flesh and dwelt among us." This is what Rev. Cornelius J. O'Connell says about Mary, the mother of God:

> Mary, although one of God's creatures like ourselves, is His holy Mother. While she is not the Mother of the Godhead, she is the Mother of the Word made flesh, who is God, equal to the Father from all eternity. Hence, she is truly the Mother of God.[27]

---

[27] O'Connell, *Holy Mary*, p. 6.

The problem is, those who deny Mary is the mother of God do not seem to understand, as O'Connell states above, that Mary is not the mother of the godhead. She is the mother of Christ who is a single person in the divine godhead. Some do not even accept Jesus as God; they should read chapter 1 of the gospel of John, which I have cited several times in this work. For example, in one part of that gospel, the Lord Jesus Himself says, "The Father and I are one" (John 10:30). If He is not God, why would He say that? Later in the same gospel, He educates Philip about His relationship with the Father:

> Jesus said to him, "Have I been with you for so long a time and you still do not know me, Philip? Whoever has seen me has seen the Father. How can you say, 'show us the Father'? Do you not believe that I am in the Father and the Father is in me? The words that I speak to you I do not speak on my own. The Father who dwells in me is doing His work." (John 14:9–10)

Clearly Jesus was telling Philip that He is God. Seeing Him, therefore, is equivalent to seeing God the Father. After reading all that Jesus has testified about Himself, why do some people maintain that Mary is not the mother of God? I truly believe what the church has taught me: Mary is the mother of Jesus Christ and at the same time the mother of God, as long as Christ is God. The Bible confirms this. The difficulty some people have is that they do not recognize Jesus as God. They regard Christ as the Son of God but not as God.

The Council of Nicaea took time to address this issue. Robert Barron addresses what trespassed in Nicaea, where Jesus Christ was declared to be one being with the Father: "Important steps were taken at the Council of Nicaea in 325, when Jesus was declared to be *homoousios* (One in being) with the Father, and at the Council of Constantinople in 381, when that teaching was reiterated."[28]

The council unequivocally declared Christ to be God. A controversy, however, arose from the teaching of Nestorius, who had been influenced by the School of Antioch, which put more emphasis on the humanity of Christ. Nestorius claimed that Christ was human and divine coming together in a moral union. To him, Mary gave birth to the human part of Jesus Christ and should therefore be called the mother of Christ. This led to a strong condemnation of this teaching: in 431 AD, "he Council at Ephesus proclaimed, 'If anyone does not confess that God is truly the Emmanuel, and that on this account the holy virgin is the "Theotokos" (for according to the flesh by birth) let him be anathema.'"

For all the reasons I have cited in this chapter, the evidence in the scriptures, and the teachings of the magisterium, Mary is the mother of God, *Theotokos*.

Mary is not only the mother of God, she is also our own mother. Let me be clear: when we call Mary our mother, we mean she is our spiritual mother, different from the biological mother who gave birth physically to Jesus Christ. Saint Paul in his epistle to the church at Colossae says that Christ "is the head of the body, the church …" (Colossians

---

[28] Barron, *Catholicism*, p. 95.

1:18). Mary is the mother of Christ, who is the head of the church; therefore, Mary is the mother of the church, which is Christ's body—the mystical body of Christ. Whoever denies this therefore denies the link between Christ and the church. Mary could not be the mother of the head without being the mother of the body. Fulton Sheen used the wedding feast at Cana to make a very interesting connection between the body of Christ and the Blessed Virgin Mary: "Cana was the death of the mother-Son relationship and the beginning of that higher love involved in the mother-humanity, Christ-redeemed relationship."[29]

In his analysis, Sheen opined that the moment the mother of Jesus approached Him about the needs of the people—"they have no wine"—asking Him to act when it was not yet His time, she adopted a new relationship: she became the mother of humanity. According to Sheen, Jesus's response, "Woman, how does your concern affect me? My hour has not yet come" (John 2:4), shows that Mary had taken on an additional role, i.e., to mother and care for the people her Son would redeem. At the wedding feast, she only presented the problem to Jesus; she did not tell Him what to do. She knew that He knew exactly what to do and was confident He would do it. He would not allow the organizers of the wedding to be embarrassed. Jesus acted because His mother asked Him to act.

She turned to the stewards, regarding them now as children who needed instruction on what to do, because they were not mature enough to deal with Jesus. She told them, "Do

---

[29] Fulton Sheen, *The World's First Love* (New York: McGraw-Hill, 2015), p. 113.

whatever He tells you." This was the beginning of His ministry through signs and wonders. Jesus protested that His "hour has not yet come," but all the same He had to oblige His mother. The power of Mary's intercession is shown in this fact: the Son who came to do the Will of the Father began by doing the will of the mother. What the Blessed Virgin Mary told the stewards was not an instruction for that moment only, but a catechesis on discipleship that would help them and every other Christian to join the new family. Later in His ministry, Jesus would refer to this family as follows: "those who hear the word of God and keep it are my brothers and sisters." Mary now was performing the role of a caring mother by making sure there was enough wine for the people and by guiding the people toward a new family. Mary's action in Cana showed not only that she was a mother who cared but also that she had intercessory powers. She solicited for her children, bringing human needs into the salvific mission of Christ. Pope Saint John Paul wrote, "Mary places herself between her Son and mankind in the reality of their wants, needs and sufferings."[30]

Mary was not just a mother but a mother who cared and interceded powerfully for her children. The Council fathers summarized the whole teaching in relation to Mary, both as the mother of God and our mother, in these words:

> She conceived, brought forth and nourished
> Christ. She presented Him to the Father in
> the temple, and was united with Him by
> compassion as He died on the Cross. In this
> singular way she cooperated by obedience,

---

[30] John Paul II, *Redemptoris Mater*, n. 21.

> faith, hope and burning charity in the work
> of the Savior in giving back supernatural
> life to souls. Wherefore she is our mother
> in the order of grace.[31]

Mary officially became our mother at the moment Jesus handed her to us, represented by John, at the foot of the cross. It is interesting to note that the sacrifice of Jesus on the cross made us God's adopted children and at the same time children of the Blessed Mother. We are her children because we are members of her son's mystical body. He identifies with us through His words and actions in the scriptures. As described in the Acts of the Apostles, Jesus appeared to Saul, who was on his way to Damascus to arrest and exterminate Christians because he thought they were a nuisance. Jesus said that by persecuting Christians, Saul was directly persecuting Him. Here is how He revealed himself to Saul:

> On his journey, as he was nearing Damascus, a light from the sky suddenly flashed around him. He fell to the ground and heard a voice saying to him, "Saul, Saul, why are you persecuting me?" He said, "Who are you, sir?" The reply came, "I am Jesus whom you are persecuting ..." (Acts 9:4–5).

Jesus saw Christians as Himself personified. And any persecution of Christians was a persecution of Him. Here He clearly identified with His Mystical Body. In the same

---

[31] *Lumen Gentium*, n. 61.

vein, His mother became the mother of His Mystical Body. On the day of the resurrection, He sent Mary Magdalene to announce the good news to His apostles: "I am going to my Father and your Father, to my God and your God" (John 20:17).

Matthew also records that on that Sunday Jesus addressed "Mary Magdalene and other Mary," who had gone to the tomb, and redefined His relationship with His apostles: "Do not be afraid. Go tell my brothers to go to Galilee, and there they will see me" (Matthew 28:10). Obviously, He was sending the women to His apostles, but He called them "my brothers." Mary lived with the apostles in the upper room as they waited for the coming of the Holy Spirit. The fact that Mary was at the inauguration of the church at Pentecost shows the role she plays in the body of Christ, the church. When God pronounced a curse on the serpent in the garden, He said, "I will put enmity between you and the woman, her seeds and your seeds." If Mary, as Pope Saint John Paul described above, is "placed at the very center of that enmity," then her seeds are no less than us, who are still struggling against the devil. Mary, therefore, is our mother, as revealed by her actions. She has played this role since the beginning of the church. After the resurrection and ascension of the Lord, she did not leave the apostles. Pope Paul VI expressed this thought in his Apostolic exhortation of May 13, 1967.

> And even after Christ had ascended to heaven she remained united to Him by a most ardent love while she faithfully fulfilled the new role of Spiritual Mother

of the most beloved of the disciples and of the nascent church.[32]

Saint Luke in the Acts of the Apostles listed the names of those who formed the first Christian community. They lived together in the upper room and included Mary, the mother of Jesus "All these," he wrote, "devoted themselves with one accord to prayers" (Acts 1:14). This confirms what His Holiness Pope Paul VI wrote about the role Mary played in the early church.

Seeing all these citations in the scripture, it would be absurd for a Christian to deny that Mary—the mother of Jesus who readily identifies with Christians—is the mother of all Christians. If, after seeing all that is written in the scriptures, one still fails to believe that Mary is the mother of God, I wonder what proof one needs. I conclude this chapter with the words of Saint Louis Marie de Montfort: "All true children of God have God for their father and Mary for their Mother; anyone who does not have Mary for his mother does not have God for his father." Jesus Christ wanted us to have both father and mother, so He handed Mary to us at Calvary.

---

[32] *Signum Magnum*, part 1,par.6.

13

Our Mother Who Art in Heaven

"I come from heaven." —The Blessed
Virgin Mary's words to the three shepherd
children in Fatima, Portugal, May 13, 1917.

Saint Therese of Lisieux, acclaimed the greatest saint of
modern times, said, "I will spend my heaven doing good on
earth." She must have been inspired by our Blessed Mother,

who has spent her time in heaven doing good for her children on earth. She watches for them and is so concerned about her children that she keeps visiting them on earth, instead of settling down in heaven to enjoy the company of angels with her divine Son. Mary could be said to have spent her time in heaven doing good on earth, because she's never stopped visiting her children. If all the Marian apparitions had been acknowledged by the church, there would be lots and lots of them on almost all the continents of the world.

The Blessed Virgin Mary was endowed with a natural instinct to be a caring and protecting mother. Naturally, mothers watch out for their children and run to their aid when there is danger. Their maternal hearts do not allow them to overlook the dangers their children may encounter or to overlook their suffering or the difficulties they go through. In most cases, children are more attached to their mothers than to any other member of the family.

Even after the end of her mortal life on earth, our Blessed Mother still cares for her children. She comes down occasionally to alert them about impending danger and to offer solutions. When God ordained that she would bear His Son, the Messiah, He also determined that His children, who would be saved by His Son, would become her children. Mary knew about this role when she was still on earth. She displayed this maternal role at the wedding in Cana, as I mentioned earlier, where she took on an intercessory role.

This role did not stop with her physical death; it continues even now. She occasionally comes down from heaven to give maternal care to her children. Almost every century since her assumption to heaven, she has visited her children in danger and showed them what to do to avert the problem. This chapter describes some of those apparitions and her messages to earth. To those who do not believe that she is in heaven, I want to mention here that she told the three shepherd children in Fatima, Portugal, in 1917, "I come from heaven," which makes her our mother who art in heaven. On December 9, 1531, the Blessed Virgin Mary appeared to Juan Diego, a newly baptized Christian, in Guadalupe and addressed him as "my little son," acknowledging her maternal status among the followers of her Son. Our mother regards even those who do not believe in her as her children. Juan Diego did not have any idea who she was, but she called him her son. She keeps visiting earth to introduce herself and to warn people who are in danger.

There have been many apparitions of our Lady since the fifteenth century. She comes from heaven to deliver messages to her children on earth. This chapter describes a few of those appearances, the ones with church approval.

Guadalupe, 1531

The first and one of the most popular apparitions of our Lady occurred in Guadalupe to Catholic convert Juan Diego. Mary appeared to a recent convert and gave him a message for the bishop. This was not intended to demean the bishop to show that she treats every one of her children equally. I'm sure there were many other devout Catholics in that place, but she appeared to this convert because she had a lesson she wanted to teach and a mission to fulfil. This shows she is real. If she had appeared to someone who was a cradle Catholic, some would have argued that it was a figment of the person's imagination due to his or her excessive devotion to Mary. But from the look of things, this man was not even a Marian devotee. When the Blessed Virgin appeared to him, he described her as a very beautiful lady. As Blessed Mary said in the Magnificat, God shows favor to the lowly. In the same way, she chose one who was a juvenile in terms of his Catholic faith.

Juan Diego was fifty-seven years old and newly baptized. His wife had died in 1529. Juan walked from his village to attend Mass in the city. On December 8, 1531, he walked his usual route to Mass. At Tepeyac Hill, near Mexico City, formerly the site of pagan temple, he saw a young, beautiful lady surrounded by light. The lady had a nice conversation with him, told him about her love for Mexico, and sent a message through him to the local bishop, Juan de Zumárraga. In the message, she directed the bishop to build a church on the spot where she'd appeared. Juan Diego went as directed and presented the message to the bishop, who understandably was very skeptical. He had reason to be apprehensive, because there had been no such apparition in the history of the church before. In addition, Juan Diego was a recent convert from paganism. There was a tendency to believe he was hallucinating.

However, the bishop asked Juan to tell the lady to give him a sign from heaven. When he reported this to the lady at their next meeting, she promised to send a sign that would convince the bishop to believe. When Juan returned home to his village, his uncle was in terrible ill health and was dying. Juan went back to the city to invite a priest to perform the last rites on his uncle. On the way he met the lady again; she told him to see the bishop instead of looking for the priest because his uncle had been healed. Juan may have been confused and nursed some doubt, but he did what the lady told him to do. She directed him to go to the hill and cut some flowers. He went and saw beautiful flowers; given that this was in December, winter, it was nothing short of a miracle.

At this point, Juan Diego may have convinced himself that he was dealing with a supernatural phenomenon. He cut the flowers and took them to the lady. She told him to take the flowers to the bishop wrapped in a mantle (*tilma*) and not show them to anyone other than the bishop. Juan was surprised when the bishop not only accepted the flowers but knelt down before the cloth, which bore a picture of the lady that Juan had not seen before. The bishop then built the church where the lady had requested. The first major effect of this apparition was that many indigenous people, who had been pagans, converted and became Christians. One miraculous sign of the Virgin of Guadalupe is that Juan Diego could pick roses in the middle of winter. In addition, the *tilma*, a poor-quality cloth made from cactus on which the image of the Virgin was imprinted, should not have lasted more than twenty years, but it survives till today and shows no sign of decay more than four hundred years after the apparitions. The unprecedented lifespan of the *tilma* defies science. The image of Our Lady of Guadalupe is on display in the Shrine of Our Lady in Guadalupe, a very popular religious site. Robert Barron writes, "And the image continues to beguile, fascinate and beckon. The Shrine of Our Lady of Guadalupe is the most visited religious site in the Christian world, surpassing Lourdes, the Church of the Holy Sepulcher and St. Peter's itself."[33]

---

[33] Barron, *Catholicism*, p. 111.

The Virgin of Guadalupe is a formidable national icon in Mexico, not only for Catholics but for all Mexicans. She is a unifying force for the people. December 12 is the feast day of Our Lady of Guadalupe, and Mexicans regard it as a national celebration.

One very interesting fact here is that the Blessed Virgin of Guadalupe visited this land when much of it was pagan. They were not active devotees of the Blessed Lady, so one cannot say her apparition was the figment of their imagination. The people then did not know about her, but today she is the most adored creature in the country. Mary prophesied this when she said "all ages will call me blessed." If this does not convince sceptics of the motherhood of the Blessed Virgin Mary, I cannot think of what would. She started with a single convert, and now the whole country is electrified by her presence. This means she is from God. Remember what Gamaliel, a teacher of the law, said about the ministry of the apostles: "For if this endeavor or activity is of human origin, it will destroy itself. But if it comes from God, you will not be able to destroy them; you may even find yourself fighting against God"(Acts 5:38–39).

Anything that is from God will stand the test of time. If a pagan people could convert, believe in God, and have so much devotion to His mother, then we have no reason to doubt that she is our mother also and working for us everywhere and all the time.

The apparition of the Virgin of Guadalupe was unique because she took a message to a virgin land. In Portugal, she would meet children saying the Rosary. Here, she appeared to a convert and sent her message to the yet-to-be converted.

Her demand for a church at the spot where she'd appeared reminds one of Jacob, who placed a stone on the spot where he'd dreamed about angels ascending and descending a ladder. That spot later became a place of worship for people.

> When Jacob awoke from his sleep, he exclaimed, "Truly, the Lord is in this spot, although I did not know it." In a solemn wonder he cried out: "How awesome is this shrine! This is nothing else but the abode of God and that is the gateway to heaven." Early the next morning Jacob took the stone that he had put under his head, set it up as a memorial stone and poured oil on top of it ... "This stone that I have set up as a memorial stone shall be God's abode." (Genesis 28:16–18, 22)

Wherever the Blessed Virgin Mary appears, the spot becomes a holy ground and "God's abode." A chapel is then built on the spot for prayers and the worship of God.

Rue de Bac, Paris, France, 1830

Our Blessed Virgin Mary is active every moment of the day, even late at night. Her apparition to Catherine Laboure clearly shows this. It was late at night on July 18, 1830, when our Lady appeared to her. She was a twenty-four-year-old novice Sister, praying in the chapel in a convent on Rue du Bac in Paris. She was in the habit of spending time in the chapel until it was late. On this night, during her prayers and meditations, our Lady appeared to her. Catherine saw the Blessed Virgin Mary descend the altar steps and sit on the chair used by the spiritual director. Here, as in Mexico, she had a message for her children in the world. Like a good, caring mother, she is always on hand to warn about impending doom. She always offers a solution. This time, she warned about the anticlericalism that would overtake the church in France. She told Catherine, "There will be bad times to come. Misfortune will come crashing down on France. The throne will be toppled. The whole world will be turned upside-down by misfortunes of all kinds." She even shed tears when she said to Catherine, There will be tears … There will be victims among the clergy of Paris; Monsignor the Archbishop will die … My child, the whole world will be plunged into gloom. On July 27, 1830, less than two weeks after Mary mentioned this to Catherine, an anticlerical revolution started in Paris. Today, it is known as the July Revolution.

Later, Mary visited Catherine in the chapel again, this time during a community meditation. Dressed in white, she stood on a globe and a golden ball. The golden ball disappeared, and she stretched out her hands inside an oval frame with golden lettering: "O Mary conceived without original sin, pray for us who have recourse to thee." As Catherine watched the apparition, she was told by an interior voice to have a medal struck with that design. The voice told her that it would be a source of great grace and should be worn on the neck. She then was shown the reverse side of the medal, which had a large letter M under a bar and cross and above two hearts, which represented the hearts of Jesus and Mary; this was circled by twelve stars. Known as the Miraculous Medal, it has become a popular icon of devotion for many people in the Catholic Church.

Following the typical Catholic tradition, Archbishop Hyacinthe-Louis de Quelen of Paris launched a canonical inquiry. He found the apparition to be authentic and so the Miraculous Medal was accepted as supernaturally inspired and responsible for genuine miracles. He therefore gave a canonical approval for devotion to the Miraculous Medal. It has become a popular symbol of devotion.

La Salette, France, 1846

On Saturday, September 19, 1846, the Blessed Virgin Mary appeared to two young children, Maximin Giraud, age eleven, and Melanie Calvat, age fourteen, while they looked after their employer's cattle on the pasture above La Salette-Fallavaux, a village near Corps. They saw a globe of light open and a lady seated on a stone with her head in her hands. They described the lady as tall and very beautiful, wearing long-sleeved dress, white and studded with pearls. She had a crown on her head. Hanging from her neck was a large crucifix adorned with a small hammer and pincers, with a brilliantly shining figure of Christ on it, they said.

She told the children that the problem of the people was their disrespect for the day of the Lord. She said, "Only a few old women go to Mass in the summer. Everyone else works every Sunday, all summer long. And in winter, when they don't know what else to do, they go to Mass only to scoff at religion. During Lent, they go to the butcher shops like dogs." This attitude, she said, annoys Jesus and makes her Son's arm heavy. "It is so heavy; I can no longer restrain it." Here, she hinted again at her powers of intervention. She asked the people to repent and obey her Son, Jesus Christ.

In most of the apparitions, the Blessed Virgin Mary calls for repentance and sometimes asks the visionaries to pray for the world to repent. This is truly in line with the message of the Lord Jesus: "Repent, for the kingdom of God is at hand."

Lourdes, France, 1858

On February 11, 1858, the Blessed Virgin Mary appeared in Lourdes to a teenage girl named Bernadette Soubirous, the first child of Francois and Louise Soubirous. The apparitions, which occurred eighteen times, put Lourdes on the map of the world. Previously, it had been a relatively unknown place. Each time the Blessed Mother appears on earth, she comes with a message. The Lourdes apparitions were similar to her other appearances around the world. In most cases, she was not known, and she sent her first message to the local church authorities. Bernadette was fourteen when the Blessed Mary appeared to her and sent a message to the priest, who as in the other cases, did not take the vision seriously. The priest sent Bernadette back to ask the heavenly visitor to identify herself. Bernadette was an unlearned young girl; she could not speak French but only her own local dialect, and she found it difficult to convince the priest that the apparition was authentic.

Bernadette's father had lost his job and subsequently his house, and the family was living in a small one-room *cachot*, a dwelling formerly used as a jail. The whole family crowded into the tiny room. On the fateful day that the lady appeared, Bernadette and her sister Toinette, age eleven, and a friend, Jeanne Abadie, age twelve, went to Massabielle on the bank of the Gave de Pau River to fetch wood. They had to cross a small stream to get to the wood on the other side. Bernadette was afraid wading through the water would trigger her asthma. She decided to wait while her sister and friend crossed the water to fetch the wood. As she waited, she heard a great noise like the sound of a storm. She left and headed toward the Grotto of Massabielle. To her shock, she saw in the opening of the rock a rosebush moving and a golden-colored cloud coming out of the grotto's interior. Immediately a young, beautiful lady emerged. This is how Bernadette described her:

> She has the appearance of young girl of sixteen or seventeen. She is dressed in a white robe, grilled at the waist with a blue ribbon which flows down all round it. A yoke closes it in graceful pleats at the base of the neck. The sleeves are long and tight-fitting. She wears upon her head a veil which is also white. This veil gives just a glimpse of her hair and falls down at the back below her waist. Her feet are bare but covered by the last fold of her robe except at the point where the yellow rose shines upon each of them. She held on her right arm a rosary of white beads with a chain of gold shining like the two roses on her feet.[34]

As the lady stood there, Bernadette took out her rosary and began to recite. The lady also had a rosary and rolled the beads through her fingers in silence as Bernadette prayed.

---

[34] Victor Cembellin, "Story of Saint Bernadette & Our Lady of Lourdes," *Medjugorje USA*, www.medjugorjeusa.org/lourdes.htm.

When Bernadette came to "glory be to the Father," the lady recited it with Bernadette. She taught Bernadette a prayer, which Bernadette recited daily till her death. As the beautiful lady did in Guadalupe, she asked Bernadette to tell the priest, Father Peyramale, to build a chapel on the site of the apparition. The priest understandably did not respond with kindness. He insisted on knowing the name of the lady. After Bernadette returned to the priest to give more information from the lady, he said, "Oh yes, you say you see visions, and you upset the whole countryside with your story. Do you know the lady's name?" He told her he would not deal with a nameless vision.

The beautiful lady spoke for the first time on February 18. She told Bernadette, "I do not promise you happiness in this world but in the other." She asked, "Would you be kind enough to come here for a fortnight?" Bernadette agreed to visit the apparition site for a fortnight. Truly, she went through a lot of suffering, particularly in the hands of government authorities who sometimes sent police to arrest Bernadette or disperse the people who gathered at the apparition site in prayer. On February 24, the lady asked Bernadette to do "penance, penance, penance" and to pray for sinners.

The authorities continued to harass Bernadette; once, they even closed the place. Bernadette's parents also stopped her from visiting the site. Many people thought she had a mental problem, but a doctor, named Dozous, who was brought in to test her confirmed that she was perfectly all right.

On March 25, the Feast of the Annunciation, the lady revealed her identity. She told Bernadette, "I am the

Immaculate Conception." The name did not mean anything to Bernadette; she did not understand what it meant. She went to the priest, repeating the name as she walked along, and told him the beautiful lady's name. When the priest heard "Immaculate Conception," he was all the more skeptical. Four years earlier, in 1854, Pope Pius IX had declared the dogma of the Immaculate Conception. The priest said to Bernadette, "The lady should have said 'I am the fruit of the Immaculate Conception,' not 'I am the Immaculate Conception.'" Bernadette insisted that she'd heard the name correctly and that was what the lady had said.

By now the site was overflowing with people. The Blessed Virgin asked her to drink water from a nearby fountain. As far as Bernadette knew, there was no fountain, but some inner impulse told her to start digging the ground with her bare hands. She noticed that the ground was moist and, before she could dig further, water started coming out. She cupped her hands to get the water and drank in the presence of the lady and every other person who was there that day.

As was true in many of the places the lady visited, her message for the world was "penance, penance, penance." She directed Bernadette to pray for sinners. Bernadette went on her knees and ate the bitter herbs that grew around the grotto for the sake of sinners.

Today, Lourdes is one of the most popular sites of our Lady's apparition; millions of pilgrims visit there yearly. Many people who go there recount healing miracles that they have experienced or witnessed. The little fountain that Bernadette dug with her hands is a sizable body of water where people wade for healing purposes, like the pool of Bethesda described in John 5:2–9.

The pilgrimage season at Lourdes begins in April and ends in October each year; the main day of the pilgrimage is the Feast of Assumption on August 15. An estimated four million to six million pilgrims from around the world make annual pilgrimages to this holy site.

Fatima, Portugal, 1917

The First World War started in the year 1914, and by early 1917 the casualties from the war had exceeded an alarming seventeen million. The war, unprecedented in human history, also wounded more than twenty million people, and there did not seem to be an end in sight. Peace was the most essential commodity needed at that time. This was during the pontificate of Pope Benedict XV, who made several appeals for peace to different quarters, to no avail. As the head of the world's Christians, whose souls were his sole responsibility, the pope believed his paramount responsibility was to bring peace to a world that faced annihilation.

In May 1917, the pope realized nothing more could be done through human efforts. He made a direct and passionate appeal to the Blessed Virgin Mary, the queen of peace, to intercede for the world peace. On May 5, 1917, the pope wrote a letter that expressed his frustration about the war and world leaders' refusal to listen to his appeal. He wrote:

> Our earnest pleading voice, invoking
> the end of the vast conflict, the suicide
> of civilized Europe, was then and has

remained ever since unheard. Indeed, it seemed that the dark tide of hatred grew higher and wider among the belligerent nations, and drew other countries into its frightful sweep, multiplying ruin and massacre. Nevertheless our confidence was not lessened … Since all graces which the Author of all good deigns to grant to the poor children of Adam by a loving design of His Divine Providence are dispensed through the hands of the most holy Virgin, we wish that the petition of most afflicted children, more than ever in this terrible hour, may turn with lively confidence to the august Mother of God.[35]

He then called on people to cry out to Mary:

To Mary, then, who is the Mother of Mercy and Omnipotent of grace, let loving and devout appeal go up from every corner of the earth, from noble temples and tiniest chapels, from royal palaces and mansions of the rich as from the poorest hut, from blood-drenched plains and seas. Let it bear to Her the anguished cry of mothers and wives, the wailing of innocent little ones, the sighs of every generous heart: that her most tender and benign solitude may

---

[35] Henry E. G. Rope, *Benedict, Pope of Peace* (London: J. Gifford Ltd., 1941), pp. 104–5.

> be moved and the peace we asked for be
> obtained for agitated world.[36]

Mary responded promptly, as the mother that she is. Just about one week after the appeal, she came down to the earth with a message of peace, promising that the war would end. Her response truly showed her motherly love and care. She appeared to three shepherd children—Lucia dos Santos, age ten, and her cousins, Francisco and Jacinta Marto, ages eight and seven, respectively. The apparition took place in Fatima, a small village about seventy miles north of Lisbon, Portugal. On May 13, 1917, these three little children took their flock to Cova da Iria. They usually recited the rosary while they watched the flock. On this day, after lunch and the rosary, they saw a bright flashing light, like lightning. The flash was followed by another one; then there was a blue sky. The children rushed the flock down the hill, thinking that it was going to rain. They were shocked and confused when a very beautiful lady stood before them on a tree, surrounded by a bright light. Lucia recalled, "A lady, clothed in white, brighter than the sun, radiating a light more clear and intense than a crystal cup filled with sparkling water, lit by burning sunlight."

Naturally the children were frightened at the sight of this mysterious lady. She smiled at them and said, "Do not be afraid, I will not harm you." Lucia, the oldest, asked her where she'd come from. The lady pointed to the sky and said, "I come from heaven." Lucia asked what she wanted. The lady said, "I have come to ask you to come here for six

---

[36] William Thomas Walsh, *Our Lady of Fatima* (New York: Doubleday, 1954), p. 49.

months on the thirteenth day of the month, at this same hour. Later, I shall say who I am and what I desire. And I shall return here yet a seventh time." She told the children, "Say the Rosary every day, to bring peace to the world and the end of the war."

She continued to appear to them on the thirteenth day of every month. Each month, she had a message for the children. Her emphasis was on prayers and penance.

On the July 13, she told the children, "Continue to come here every month. In October I will tell you who I am and what I want, and I will perform a miracle for all to see and believe. Sacrifice yourselves for sinners, and say many times, especially when you make some sacrifice, 'O Jesus, it is for love of you, for the conversion of sinners, and in reparation for the sins committed against the Immaculate Heart of Mary.'" At that point, she showed them a vision of hell. In the words of Lucia, hell was "full of demons and lost souls amidst indescribable terrors." Afterward, she told the children, "When you pray the Rosary, say after each mystery, 'O my Jesus, forgive us, save us from the fire of hell. Lead all souls to heaven, especially those who are in need.'" This prayer has since become part and parcel of the Rosary. You can be sure the children were eager to pray to save people from the torture they had just witnessed in that vision of hell.

On August 13, civil authorities prevented the children from visiting the apparition site as the lady had requested. By now the apparition had attracted the attention of many people, and a large crowd gathered at the site. The children were confined and threatened for two days, but they were ready to give up their lives rather than betray the promises they made to the lady. They were released. On August 19, while they were feeding their flock in a place called Yalinhos, the lady visited them again. Lucia asked what she wanted from them, and she said, "I want you to continue to go to Cova da Iria on the thirteenth so that you may continue to say the Rosary every day. I, in the last month, will make a miracle that all will believe." Then, with a very sad face, she told them, "Pray, pray very much, and make sacrifices for sinners; for many souls go to hell, because there are none to sacrifice for them and pray for them."

On September 13, she urged them keep saying the Rosary to ensure the end of the war. She revealed to them that Jesus and Saint Joseph would accompany her in October to bless the world. Lucia petitioned her to cure some people, to which the lady responded, "Yes, I will cure some, but not others. In October I will perform a miracle so that all may believe." At this point, a lot of people were very skeptical about the apparition. They needed a miracle to be convinced.

October 13, 1917

The promise of public miracle by the lady increased the number of people who visited the apparition site in October. People came from other parts of the country. Some were skeptics who came to ridicule everything, including representatives from the antireligious newspaper *O Seculo.* The Blessed Mary appeared, and Lucia asked her, for the last time, what she wanted. She responded, "I want to tell you that a chapel is to be built here in my honor. I am the Lady of the Rosary. Continue always to pray the Rosary every day.

The war will end, and the soldiers will soon return to their homes." Lucia reported that the Blessed Mother grew very sad and said, "Do not offend the Lord our God anymore, because He is already so much offended."

As she said these words, she rose into midair and, opening her hands toward the sun, she disappeared. The sun now glowed more brilliantly. She was replaced by various visions that only the children could see. The vast crowd that was present witnessed a true miracle. The sun that was so brilliant turned into a dull gray disc into which everybody could look directly. The antireligious newspaper adopted a very different tone from its earlier satirical article about Fatima:

> ... one could see the immense multitude turn towards the sun, which appeared free from clouds at its zenith. It looked like a plaque of dull silver and it was possible to look at it without the least discomfort. It might have been eclipse which was taking place. But at that moment a great shout went up, and one could hear the spectators nearest at hand shouting, "A miracle! A miracle!" Before the astonished eyes of the crowd, whose aspect was biblical as they stood bareheaded, eagerly searching the sky, the sun trembled, made a sudden incredible movement outside all cosmic laws—the sun "danced," according to the typical expression of the people ... [37]

---

[37] www.theotokos.org.uk/pages/approved/appariti/fatima.html

We can see that the newspaper's editors came to believe that something "outside all cosmic laws" had happened at Fatima.

In the story of our salvation, there is something interestingly similar about shepherds and messages from heaven. In the Old Testament, God appeared to Moses while he was shepherding his father-in-law's flock. The first humans to hear news of the birth of Christ were shepherds in the field minding their sheep. Many years later in Fatima, Portugal, the Blessed Mother appeared to three little shepherd children, identifying herself as coming from heaven. While her first message was about the salvation of the world, the second advocated for the peace in the world. Like the angel from heaven, she assured the children not to be afraid for she would not harm them. Her message was motherly advice about how to restore peace in the world and appease the Lord Jesus, who had been greatly offended by the people of the world. The little children were to spread her message. In what is now known as the World Apostolate of Fatima, the message continues to spread.

In conclusion, we know that she gave birth to Christ through the power of the Holy Spirit; we as Christians are members of the Mystical Body of Christ, which makes us her children by adoption. Jesus Christ prayed to the Father for this spiritual family, which is the seed of the woman positioned against the seed of the evil one in Genesis: "her seed and your seed." In the gospel of John, Jesus says:

> I pray not only for them, but also for those who will believe in me through their words. So that they may all be one, as you,

> Father are in me and I in you, that they also
> may be in us, that the world may know that
> you sent me … I in them and you in me,
> that they may be brought to perfection as
> one … (John 17:20–21, 23)

This is what we say in the Preface of the Fourth Sunday of Lent, Year A: "By the mystery of the Incarnation, He has led the human race that walked in darkness into the radiance of faith and has brought those born in slavery to ancient sin through the waters of regeneration to make them your adopted children." Through Him, we have become God's adopted children.

While He hung on the cross on Calvary, the Lord Jesus handed Mary over to John, saying, "Mother behold your son, son behold your mother." The scripture tells us that John took her into his home. She became not just a mother to John but to the other apostles as well. She was there when the Holy Spirit was sent to the Apostles. Mary had the singular privilege to have had a double shower of the Holy Spirit; the first time was at the annunciation.

The apparition of Our Lady of Fatima is also one of the most popular apparition stories of the Virgin Mary in the history of the Catholic Church. This is probably because of the history behind the apparition, the intervention of the Virgin Mary as the mother of peace. When she is addressed as the queen of peace, she truly shows herself to be one. She came when the world was at the brink of collapse because of the First World War and delivered peace through the recitation of the Rosary.

14

Mary, the Teacher and Evangelizer

A teacher imparts knowledge—formal or informal—to another individual. The informal lessons, in most cases, are cultural and come from either a parent or a peer. Mary, the mother of Christ, also was His informal teacher. She and Joseph brought Him up in the religious culture of their people. They took Him on a pilgrimage to the temple when He was of age. Mary was also an evangelizer, as seen at the wedding feast in Cana.

Mary speaks only six times in the scriptures, but her statements have deep meaning and create lasting memories. Each statement conveys a very important message. One of the most important was the instruction she gave to the stewards at the wedding feast: "Do whatever He tells you" (John 2:5). Those are the last spoken words of the Blessed Virgin Mary recorded in the scriptures. As Pope Francis puts it, that they are the legacy that she leaves to all of us. It is the way of life of the people of God. Did she purposely hold these words back so they would be her final words to her children? It may just be a coincidence, but God knows how to program things to fulfill His will.

Just as most mothers are their children's first teachers, Mary teaches her children how to receive gifts and blessings from God through obedience to Christ. She began teaching people about the will of God at the wedding. Mary had pondered all the events of Christ's life in her heart, and by this point she had also learned a lot about her Son. It was now time to teach her would-be children how to receive God's favors. She gave instructions on how to obtain a miracle from Christ. When the Blessed Mother told the stewards "do whatever He tells you," she was just echoing what God the Father said at the transfiguration: "This is my beloved Son, with whom I am well pleased, listen to Him" (Matthew 17:5). Moses also told the people of Israel, "A prophet like me will the Lord, your God, raise up for you from among your kinsmen; to him you shall listen" (Deuteronomy 18:15). Mary was repeating what God and the leading Old Testament figure had said. Interestingly, the Father and the Mother were saying the same thing about the Son. As a matter of necessity, we must listen to Him.

These three exhortations point to Jesus as the person who must be obeyed if we are to get to heaven. Jesus Christ Himself said, "My sheep hear my voice, I know them and they follow me" (John 10:27). The Blessed Mother leads us to Christ and instructs us how to be true followers: "Do what He tells you." It is therefore not correct to say that our devotion to Mary distracts us from following Christ and giving Him due honor. In most cultures of the world, the influence of the mother on a child is enormous, and the child depends on the mother because she knows his or her needs better than any other person. Most children are more attached to their mothers than their fathers because of the mother's natural role. The role mothers play is in their nature as women; they are very caring and protecting.

If the world had heeded her instruction to do what Jesus tells us, like the stewards did at the wedding feast, there certainly would have been a substantial change in the lives of Christians—from the water of chaos to the wine of pleasure—and peace would reign throughout the world. If the servers at the marriage feast had not listened to the advice of the Blessed Mother, if they had questioned her authority or argued about whether to obey her, there would have been chaos. Unfortunately, that is what is happening today; many Christians question the authority of the Blessed Virgin Mary and refuse to give her the respect she is due. As a consequence, we drive away her caring touch, which led to Jesus's first miracle, turning water into wine. Until Christians acknowledge the role of the Blessed Virgin Mary and honor her, we shall always miss her intercessory role in our lives. This, however, will not deter her from praying and interceding for her children and constantly visiting the world to help them do what God wants them to do.

"Do whatever He tells you." Mary was calling the new generation of followers of Christ to make the same commitment the people of Israel made when God spoke to them through Moses, and they all answered, "We will do everything that the Lord has told us" (Exodus 24:3). Mary calls on the people to follow the new Moses to the Promised Land, the heavenly Jerusalem, as their fathers followed the Old Testament Moses.

Today, there are many Christians but not as many true followers of Christ, in the real sense of the word. Many Christians do not do whatever He asks of them. Saint James addressed this idea of not keeping to the Word and offered this advice to Christians:

> Be doers of the word and not hearers only, deluding yourselves. For if anyone is hearer of the word and not a doer, he is like a man who looks at his own face in the mirror. He sees himself, then goes off and promptly forgets what he looked like. (James 1:22–24)

This is exactly what is going on in contemporary Christianity. There are churches around every corner. Both mainstream media outlets and social media have been fully utilized to preach the gospel; yet the world is still not what God wants it to be. Rather, there is so much hatred, class division, gender bias, and ethnic segregation everywhere, more now than ever before. Many Christians are hearers of the Word, not doers. Jesus calls for genuine love among His followers, but instead there is hatred everywhere. Many people go to Church but remain as they were before, without a positive change of heart or lifestyle. Saint James accurately compares them to a man who looks in the mirror and forgets what he's seen. No matter what the minister of the gospel says from the pulpit, modern Christians listen, but then the whole sermon "evaporates" from their hearts and minds. Little wonder that people go to church, listen to sermons by the most eloquent preachers, and pay their tithes with promptness. Yet in their relations with people, they still are guided, not by the universal law of love as taught by Jesus

Christ, but by ethnic, class, gender, or political ideologies. Those who do not belong in the same group as they do are seen as the "other." James is right. To hear the word of God and keep it is the watch word. "Do whatever He tells you."

In all the apparitions of the Blessed Virgin Mary, she is always encouraging Christians, and indeed everybody, to please God and His Son, Jesus Christ. She plays the role of an evangelizer, always trying to bring people closer to God. She does not want people to die in sin. She always calls for repentance, knowing that God does not want people to die as sinners, as He said through the mouth of the prophet Ezekiel: "'Do I indeed derive any pleasure from the death of the wicked?' says the Lord God. 'Do I not rather rejoice when he turns from his evil way that he may live?'" (Ezekiel 18:23).

God is pleased when an evildoer, a sinner, repents, so Mary always pleaded for sinners to repent and turn away from their sins to please the Lord. She even asked the visionaries to pray and offer sacrifices for sinners, as she did in Fatima, Portugal, when she told the children, "Pray, pray very much, and make sacrifices for sinners …" In Lourdes, she told Bernadette, "Penance, penance, penance," then directed her to "kiss the ground on behalf of sinners." She always said how much her Son has been offended and always pleaded for repentance.

Repentance is the message that Jesus always gave to the people. "Do you think that because these Galileans suffered in this way they were greater sinners than all other Galileans? By no means! But I tell you, if you do not repent, you will all perish as they did" (Luke 13:2–3). From what I have cited above, we can see that the Blessed Virgin Mary has the same mission as God and His Son, Jesus Christ. She wants the salvation of our souls. Those who argue that devotion to Mary distracts us from the true worship of God are not correct. If anything, devotion to Mary leads us to a perfect relationship with Christ and God the Father. The Blessed Mother, in addition to her natural maternal role, also plays the role of a preacher, an evangelizer leading people to God through her Son Jesus Christ.

It is interesting to see Mary taking on the role John the Baptist played as he prepared the people for God, calling on them to repent to avert His wrath. At the wedding feast in Cana, she played the double role of intercessor and preacher. When she said there was a shortage of wine at the feast, she was an intercessor; then she turned to the stewards and told them, "Do what He tells you." She was basically saying, "Obey Him." Obedience to Christ is the essential Christian teaching. "Do what He tells you" is essential evangelization mantra. It has become the philosophy of Christian life— doing the will of our Lord Jesus, who said, "If you love me you will keep my commandments." (John 14:15). The Lord Jesus later showed that listening to and obeying Him has a whole chain reaction and leads to a durable relationship with the divine godhead. He said, "Whoever loves me will keep my word, and my Father will love him, and we will come to him and make our dwelling with him" (John 14:23). He even extended this teaching to those who would later preach in His name; here is what He told His apostles: "Whoever listens to you listens to me. Whoever rejects you rejects me. And whoever rejects me rejects the one who sent me" (Luke 10:16).

The Blessed Mother, therefore, is working with the Father and the Son to bring forth our salvation. The Blessed Mother even asked the visionaries to pray for sinners. This again is a very strong lesson on the intercessory role of the saints, in which Catholics believe, although they are criticized by non-Catholics. If she who lives in heaven could ask these visionaries—who were blessed to see her in person—to pray for sinners, that can mean only one thing: from her place in heaven, she has seen the power of intercession held by the holy ones, who plead before God on behalf of humans on earth. And God listens.

At the end of our earthly lives, we shall be judged on how much we were able to do whatever Jesus told us to do. We have many such commands in the scriptures, the most outstanding one is "I give you a new commandment: love one another. As I have loved you, so you also should love one another" (John 13:34). Mary has played a very good role as a teacher and an evangelizer to educate her children on what to do to enter the kingdom of heaven. It is left for us to heed her call and do what Jesus has told us to do, that is, to love one another.

15

Do Catholics Worship Mary?

> Let those who think that the Church pays
> too much attention to Mary give heed to
> the fact that Our Lord Himself gave ten
> times as much of His life to her as He gave
> to His Apostles.[38]

It is no secret that many Christians do not support devotion to the Blessed Virgin Mary. Some accuse Catholics of idolatry when we offer devotion to Mary. I have always told people that if they are going to accuse Catholics of idolatry because of our devotion to the Blessed Virgin, they should start with God, who sent the angel Gabriel to Mary. They should accuse the angel who gave Mary heavenly greetings and said how blessed she was because she'd found favor with God. That action showed us that we should give her respect. Archbishop Fulton Sheen analyzed the greeting, which shows that honoring Mary is not out of place since the heavenly creature sent by God had honored her first:

---

[38] Fulton Sheen, *The World's First Love* (Garden City, New York: Doubleday, 1956), p. 88.

An angel salutes a woman! This would be a perversion of Heaven's order, worse than men's worshipping animals, unless Mary had been destined by God to be even greater than the angels—aye, their very Queen! And so the angel who was accustomed to be honored by men, now honors the woman. This ambassador of God gives no order but salutes her: "Hail, full of grace." "Hail" is our English translation for the Greek *Chaire* and probably is the equivalent of the old Aramaic formula *Shalom,* which meant "Rejoice" or "Peace be to you." "Full of grace," the rare word in the Greek gospel, signifies either "most gracious" or "full of virtue." It was almost like a proper noun in which God's emissary affirms that she is the object of His Divine pleasure."[39]

The accusations leveled against Catholics by our non-Catholic brethren say that we worship Mary. Do we truly worship Mary? That is very far from the truth. The Catholic Church does not worship Mary. The church teaches that the only being we should worship is God, and He is the only one we worship in the Catholic Church. Mary, by virtue of her elevated place among humans and her role in salvation history, has been honored since God sent the angel Gabriel to deliver the great message of the birth of His Son, Jesus.

Our Lord Jesus Christ gave His mother the respect and honor she was due here on earth; the scripture tells us that

---

[39] Sheen, *The World's First Love,* 2015 p. 52.

"He was obedient to them," a reference to Mary and Joseph At the marriage feast in Cana, He addressed her as "woman," but due to her intercession, He worked the miracle He had not yet intended to perform. Finally, He entrusted her to the care of one of His apostles. It was His last act of respect and honor to His mother on earth.

The woman "from the crowd" in the public arena where Jesus was speaking did not know the Blessed Virgin, but she poured blessings on Mary, telling her Son: "Blessed is the womb that carried you and the breasts at which you were nursed" (Luke 11:27). The Lord Jesus was quick to respond: "Rather, blessed are those who hear the word of God and observe it."(Luke 11:28). Here, Mary is blessed by Jesus because she'd heard and observed the word of God, brought to her by the angel, without which the Lord Jesus would not have spoken to the crowd and amazed the woman who spoke out. This recalls what Elizabeth said to Mary: "Blessed are you who believe that what was spoken to you by the Lord would be fulfilled" (Luke 1:45).

Honoring Mary did not start with us; it started with the annunciation. We are only fulfilling the inspired utterance of the Blessed Virgin Mary, stated in the Magnificat: "from henceforth all ages will call me blessed." She was speaking through the influence of the Holy Spirit. She then knew that people would honor her because of the great things God has done for her. From the citations above, we know that Blessed Mary was adored and blessed in the scriptures well before the current generation. There is nothing wrong with giving honor to whom honor is due. Like many others, Rev. Cornelius J. O'Connell believes "We would fail in our duty to God if we did not give to His holy Mother the respect and honor that she deserves."[40] We are obliged to honor her because God honored her first.

The honor we give to Mary does not in any way diminish the honor we give to God or our Lord Jesus Christ, as some people erroneously believe. As a matter of fact, we honor Mary because she gave birth to Christ, our Savior. As Fulton Sheen wrote, "It is on account of Our Divine Lord that Mary receives special attention, and not on account of herself."[41] If God had not chosen her to give birth to Christ, she would have been just like any other woman. Sheen expressed this when he said, "It is because Our Lord is so different from other sons that we set His Mother apart from other Mothers." Her greatness comes from the greatness of God, who was the first to honor her. When we honor Mary, we are giving glory to God, who honored her first by making her the Mother of His Son. Scott Hahn sums it up this way: "What, after all, did Mary ever *do* to *earn* such honor from God? All her good works flowed from His graces. Thus all honor and glory belong to God."[42] That is why she glorified Him in the Magnificat: "The almighty has done great things for me; holy is His name." We as her children honor her because, of all created beings, she is the most favored. She had the singular honor of giving birth to God. She sang God's praises when she said, "from hence forth all ages will call me blessed." It is interesting to note that even the Koran discusses the Blessed Virgin Mary, confirming her prediction that all ages would call her blessed. We do not worship Mary; we only honor her.

---

[40] O'Connell, *Holy Mary*, p. 8.

[41] Sheen, *The World's First Love*, p. 40.

[42] Hahn, *Hail, Holy Queen*, p. 133.

The only person to whom we give our total worship is God. The saints are given the honor they are due because of their places in heaven. The three words that differentiate these types of honor are *latria*, *dulia*, and *hyperdulia*. *Latria* is the honor due to God alone; no human being deserves such honor. *Dulia* is honor given to human beings such as the saints. *Hyperdulia* is the honor given only to Mary as the mother of Christ. When people do not know the difference, they make the mistake of believing that these words mean one and the same.

The Blessed Virgin is honored by humans because God has done great things for her; when we honor her, we join her in saying "holy is His name." In honoring her, we honor God, who created her, made her holy, and blessed her with abundance of grace. She is not like any other created being, because God favored her from her birth, which the angel told her about during the annunciation. When we honor Mary, we acknowledge God's greatness in making a woman worthy of giving her flesh to the Word of God. Saint Bernard of Clairvaux said, "Let us not imagine that we obscure the glory of the Son by the great praise we lavish on the Mother; for the more she is honored, the greater is the glory of her Son. There can be no doubt that whatever we say in praise of the Mother gives praise to the Son." Those who make the mistake of thinking that to honor Mary is to take away honor from God or His Son should listen to Saint Bernard.

If we ignored her, that would mean we were not fulfilling the prophecy of the Blessed Virgin Mary. Rather, we'd be living the other aspect of the curse that was placed on the serpent: "I will put enmity between you and the woman, her seed and your seed." Those who honor Mary are truly her seed, and those who hate to honor her may not have any other reason other than that they are the seeds of the serpent. At Fatima, the Blessed Mother lamented the lack of honor for her immaculate heart. She said, "When my immaculate heart triumphs, the world will have peace."

Pope Saint John Paul said, "For it must be recognized that before anyone else it was God himself, the eternal Father, who entrusted Himself to the Virgin of Nazareth, giving her His own Son in the mystery of the incarnation."[43] This alone should convince us that she is worthy of honor. The evil one, who is always on the opposing side, will continue to confuse his own seed with flimsy reasons for not honoring such an honorable woman, who is the most highly favored one among all humans and the most blessed among all women. Those who recognize her as their mother will always honor her and call her blessed, because this is the fulfillment of her inspired statement: "all ages will call me blessed."

Isn't it interesting? Those who criticize the Catholic Church for honoring Mary claim to know the Bible very well. Yet they fail to note that nowhere in all of scripture does an angel say "hail" to any human being except Mary. Doesn't that make her special?

---

[43] Jason Evert, *Saint John Paul the Great: His Five Loves* (Lakewood, CO: Totus Tuus Press, 2014), p. 169.

SELECT REFERENCES

Barron, Robert. *Catholicism: A Journey to the Heart of the Faith.* New York: Image Books, 2011.

Emmerich, Anne Catherine. *The Life of the Blessed Virgin Mary.* Translated by Sir Michael Palairet. Charlotte, NC: Tan Books, NC, 2011.

Evert, Jason. *Saint John Paul the Great: His Five Loves.* Lakewood, CO: Totus Tuus Press, 2014.

Francis . *Encountering Truth: Meeting God in the Everyday.* New York: Image Books, 2015.

Hahn, Scott. *Hail, Holy Queen: The Mother of God in the Word of God.* New York: Image Books, 2001.

John Paul II. *Redemptoris Mater.* March 25, 1987.

Lumen Gentium. November 21, 1964.

Paul VI. *Signum Magnum.* May 13, 1967.

O'Connell, Cornelius J. *Holy Mary: Getting To Know and Love Our Blessed Mother Through Her Magnificent Titles.* Baltimore, MD: John Murphy Company, 2016.

Rope, Henry E. G. *Benedict, Pope of Peace.* London: J. Gifford Ltd., 1941.

Sheen, Fulton J. *Life of Christ.* New York: Image Books, 1990.

————. *The World's First Love: Mary, Mother of God.* Abridged ed. San Francisco, Ignatius Press, 2015.

Stapples, Tim. *Behold Your Mother: Biblical and Historical Defense of the Marian Doctrines.* El Cajon, CA: Catholic Answers, Inc., 2014.

Walsh, William Thomas. *Our Lady of Fatima.* New York: Doubleday, 1954.

Glory to Jesus!

Honor to Mary!

Ave Maria!

Printed in the United States
By Bookmasters